PENGUIN BOOKS
# WHEN BLACKBIRDS SING

Martin Boyd was born in Switzerland in 1893 of Anglo-Australian parents. He was brought to Australia when six months old where the Boyd family made impressive contributions to the artistic and intellectual life. At the outbreak of the first world war he travelled to England and joined an English regiment and later the Royal Flying Corps. In 1948, at the height of his literary success, he returned to Australia to make a permanent home near Berwick.

Most of his novels maintain an Anglo-Australian theme and are based on his preoccupation with his own family. Martin Boyd moved to Rome in 1957 and lived there till his death in June 1972.

# BY MARTIN BOYD

### FICTION

*Love Gods* (1925)
*Brangane: A Memoir* (1926)
*The Montforts* (1928, revised edition, 1963)
*Scandal of Spring* (1934)
*The Lemon Farm* (1935)
*The Picnic* (1937)
*Night of the Party* (1938)
*Nuns in Jeopardy* (1940)
*Lucinda Brayford* (1946, revised edition, 1954)
*Such Pleasure* (1949)

### THE LANGTON QUARTET (in reading order)

*The Cardboard Crown* (1952, revised edition, 1964)
*A Difficult Young Man* (1955)
*Outbreak of Love* (1957)
*When Blackbirds Sing* (1962)

*The Tea-Time of Love* (1969)

### AUTOBIOGRAPHIES

*A Single Flame* (1939)
*Day of My Delight: An Anglo-Australian Memoir* (1965)

### NON-FICTION

*Much Else in Italy: A Subjective Travel Book* (1958)

### CHILDREN'S NOVEL

*The Painted Princess: A Fairy Story* (1936)

# Martin Boyd

# WHEN BLACKBIRDS SING

## With an introduction by Dorothy Green

PENGUIN BOOKS

Penguin Books Australia Ltd,
487 Maroondah Highway, P.O. Box 257
Ringwood, Victoria, 3134, Australia
Penguin Books Ltd,
Harmondsworth, Middlesex, England
Penguin Books,
40 West 23rd Street, New York, N.Y. 10010, U.S.A.
Penguin Books Canada Ltd,
2801 John Street, Markham, Ontario, Canada
Penguin Books (N.Z.) Ltd,
182-190 Wairau Road, Auckland 10, New Zealand

First published by Abelard-Schuman, 1962
Published by Penguin Books Australia, 1984

Copyright © Martin Boyd, 1962
Copyright © Guy Boyd, 1972

Made and printed in Hong Kong by
LP & Associates

**CIP**

Boyd, Martin, 1893-1972.
When blackbirds sing.

First published: London: Abelard-Schuman, 1962.
ISBN 0 14 006905 4.

I. Title.

A823'.2

# INTRODUCTION

Few modern Australian writers can have directed such savage, pointed criticism, in books and in letters to newspapers, at the leaders of State, Church and the professions as Martin Boyd. He denounced in print Lloyd George, Baldwin and Churchill, generals and newspaper tycoons. He wrote furious letters to two Archbishops of Canterbury and recorded his disillusionment with a third. His letters to Archbishop Temple on the saturation bombing of Hamburg and Dresden do not suggest that the cleric got the best of the argument. Boyd, for one thing, had first-hand experience of the appalling trench warfare of the first world war, as well as his service with the Royal Flying Corps at a time when the British were losing fifty pilots in training a day. Few critics indeed who wrote with such controlled passion have had their criticisms so abundantly vindicated by subsequent history and the work of professional historians.

Boyd's most important fiction, *Lucinda Brayford*, the four Langton novels, underpinned by the two versions of his autobiography, *A Single Flame* and *Day of My Delight* each describe a great arc, an emblem of the tragedy of our times: the movement to total disillusionment with authority. In his boyhood and youth, within his own family and at school in Melbourne, Boyd heard the voice of authority as the voice of the Good, its commands based on reason and justice. From 1914 onwards, after the old men of Europe had either murdered, or wrecked the lives of, a whole generation of young people, the voice of authority sounded to him like the voice of Evil. The second world war, the Depression between wars, Korea,

Vietnam, none of the consequences which flowed from the first European 'civil war', did anything to change his view. A considerable part of his energy as a man and an artist was devoted to preventing the further slaughter of a generation of youth. By then of course, the nature of war and its targets had changed.

This is not an aspect of Boyd's work which receives much critical attention. Society does not like to hear about what Boyd called 'the sickness at the top'. It is not indeed the first aspect of his work which strikes a reader new to his novels, though it is present in his most ephemeral pot-boilers. One cannot help being carried along by the easy flow of the narrative, the atmosphere of leisured enjoyment and social sophistication, the constant shimmer of wit and sheer fun, even against a darkening background, the brief but exquisite glimpses of the natural world at whichever end of the globe his Anglo-Australian characters happen to be at the moment. The people he writes about belong mainly to a social group living in what might be called fortunate circumstances, and that conditions us to believe we are reading about fortunate circumstances. It is a shock to look back at the work as a whole and realize that we have been reading about the disappearance of reason, truth and justice from the public life of the Western world. The little enclave of colonial gentry in the Langton novels, always slightly out of step with their society, are really a microcosm of European civilization in the classic sense; their hereditary connections with English branches of their family simply make the point clearer. What happened to this forgotten group of emigrants in Port Phillip from the 1840s and 1850s onwards, their displacement as leaders of Melbourne society by Western-district graziers, their engulfment by the cosmopolitan adventurers of the gold-rushes, was a pale portent of what was to be repeated in the tragic mode in Europe between 1914 and 1918, leaving power in the hands of those who had no concept of responsibility either to the land or to the future.

Hardly any American or British readers today and few Australians are aware that Australia ever had such a class of emigrants as they meet in Boyd's novels; these novels, indeed, have done most to keep their memory alive. Martin Boyd once remarked that the British were interested in Australia only when there was a war on; the observation provides more than one occasion for satire in these novels. Certainly many educated Australians even today are surprised when they go to work or study in England or America at how little their kinsmen know about this country, and, in the case of the British, how little they wish to know. If the British have an image of Australians at all, it is a distorted one acquired from the Australian comedian Barry Humphries, implying that Sydney and Melbourne are populated by male and female Dame Edna Everages. It is rare for an Englishman who has not visited Australia to know that its capital is Canberra. A few have some dim memory that Australia was the place to which England once sent its convicts, but the implications of the fact for themselves are lost on them. The Americans know little more, but, from mixed motives, display more willingness to find out. They however never refer to the fact that the American colonies had a much longer association with the convict system than Australia did, one no less cruel.

Australians have never helped to dispel these historical falsifications. They have been so much in love with their homespun equalitarianism that they have ignored the small, but valuable, contribution to their culture made by the younger sons, or cadet branches of 'good families', the occasional royal bastards under assumed names, the members of the 'acceptable' professions and their wives, without which the tapestry of Australian history would lack a rich thread. The best way to assess this contribution is to imagine what Australia might have been like if it had not been made. There would then have been no antidote at all to the ethic of Calvinist utilitarianism that prevailed in the middle classes, which, like their counterparts in Britain, believed that riches were a sign of godliness. Like every other type of emigrant, the 'gentry' wished to better themselves financially, and in some cases used methods of doing so which did them little credit. But they did not automatically put money before everything else, as the class that displaced them did, and this was one of the reasons the gentry found it hard to survive, unless they were willing to marry into the commercial classes. Individuals might fall short, but as a class they were the bearers of values, which however attenuated they had become, were in origin Renaissance-Greek. One of these values was a code of civilized behaviour which made for ease of intercourse in social life, a code which they adapted with considerable tact to new social conditions. It was as if the wide cloudless skies and the brilliant sunlight of the country itself had rid the English conventions of their stuffiness and left that endearing mixture of order and informality, which characterizes, or used to characterize, some of the older Australian station homesteads. Boyd draws a contrast, for instance, in *Outbreak of Love* between the simple ease of manners of the governors of the early days compared with the increasing taste for pomp and ceremony of their twentieth-century counterparts.

The main opposition set up in each of Boyd's principal novels is between those who do things simply because they take pleasure in them and those who do things from some other motive, because it will advance their career, or push them up the social ladder, or because 'it is good for them'. One consequence of not having as a rule to work for a living, is that one can work at what one enjoys and this encourages the belief that life was meant to be enjoyed. The idea that the world was beautiful and we were meant to enjoy living in it was for Boyd a primary distinction between the aristocrat and the bourgeois. The characters he most admires are most often to be seen taking pleasure in one another's company, at picnics, sketching parties, home-made amusements; sharpening their wits on one another at dinner, listening to music, swimming, wandering in the bush, all without any sense that time matters. The idea that time is money is absent from Boyd's scale of values and its rejection is part of the search for truth he is conducting in these novels. His purpose is to analyse ruthlessly what was left of permanent worth in the aristocratic tradition he had been brought up to respect, an analysis he brings to an unexpected conclusion in the novel *Such Pleasure*, the story of a snobbish woman intent on reaching the top of the social ladder; a character, he said, who was based on the short-story writer Barbara Baynton.

Boyd's subject matter has inevitably led to misunderstanding and accusations of snobbishness. His notions of class were entirely his own, vertical not horizontal, according to his half-serious division between Right and Left in *The Cardboard Crown*. On the Right were all the people who liked their work, quite apart from the money it brought in: farmers, artists, craftsmen, musicians, sailors, clergymen. On the Left were all those to whom money was of supreme importance, stock-brokers, businessmen, anyone who believed that 'living matter was something they could control like a machine', for profit. What he ultimately valued in people, as he did in books, was the degree of their humanity. 'Good birth' counted for little with him if lovingkindness was absent. One of his most sympathetic portraits, for example, occurs in an early novel *Dearest Idol*. The most attractive and intelligent character in the book is the young wife, kind, straightforward and without pretentiousness, the daughter of a self-made rich man of no education. Beside her, her 'gentleman' husband cuts a poor figure. Another instance is the treatment of Helena's bourgeois father Bert Craig, in *A Difficult Young Man*, whose simplicity and humane feeling give him his high moment of tragic dignity. The real targets of Boyd's satire are the dishonest, the hypocritical and above all, the cruel. Snobbishness, by contrast, is venial, since at least it has an element of aspiration in it, ignoble though it may be.

Intertwined with his examination of the 'aristocratic' is Boyd's analysis of the role of heredity in human behaviour, a major theme in *The Montforts, Lucinda Brayford* and the Langton novels. His aim was to reveal the persistence of hereditary traits, over long periods of time, and to suggest the possibility of inheriting similar patterns of experience, as in the case of Alice Langton and her daughter, Diana, who are both exploited by the men they love. All the material he needed was at his hand in the family he was born into. He said once, it appeared to him that when he was young the world was composed entirely of his relatives. His father's family, the Boyds, and his mother's, the à Becketts, formed a numerous and close-knit tribe. Ancient and distinguished on both sides, the à Becketts in particular retained in the colonies an inherited streak of rebellious eccentricity, combined with an artistic talent which sometimes amounted to genius. They also had a highly developed sense of the ridiculous and a ready wit; one of Boyd's great-uncles helped to found London *Punch*. In the remote family background, a collateral connection with St Thomas à Beckett 'hung like a glittering ornament on the family tree', while on his father's side was a distant connection with Dean Swift. The Boyd ancestors, Irish aristocrats of Scottish origin, played a turbulent part in history, but during the eighteenth century

married women who brought a rich gift into the family: great pain-
terly ability combined with scientific curiosity, which has endured
to this day. One of Boyd's cousins was a biologist who became the
first woman lecturer at the University of Melbourne; in the art
world, the name 'Boyd' in Australia today is a household word.
Arthur and Guy Boyd, Martin's nephews, have overseas reputations
as painter and sculptor; their younger brother David is equally well-
known as potter and painter, and the younger generations are
making their mark in many directions, including music. The late
Robin Boyd, another nephew, was one of Australia's most famous
architects, a profession for which Martin himself was training before
the first war.

From his mother's side of the family, which included a long line
of judges, barristers, and Victoria's first Chief Justice, Martin Boyd
inherited a passion for reason and justice, and a disconcerting logic
which could still disturb a dinner-table, when he was well into his
seventies.

Boyd's father, Arthur Merric Boyd, and his mother, Emma à
Beckett, were both fine painters, and their children all grew up in
an atmosphere in which it was as natural to paint and sketch as to
breathe. As described in *The Cardboard Crown*, his eldest brother died
young; the next brother William Merric was justly known as the
'father of Australian pottery'; his wife, Doris Gough, was his partner
in this enterprise.

Boyd's father and mother appear in the Langton novels as 'Steven'
and 'Laura', the father a somewhat remote, but extremely just figure,
with enlightened views about child-rearing. The mother was a
beautiful, highly gifted woman, and deeply religious, a trait she
passed on to her son Merric and to Martin. She is drawn perhaps
in more detail as Susan, in *The Montforts*, an early novel in which

Boyd felt he had made inadequate use of his material. This is not quite true: *The Montforts* has its own special attraction, especially its account of pre-goldrush society, and in softening some of the portraits later, Boyd lost a little of their clarity. His brother, Merric, is to some extent the model for Dominic in the Langton novels. The reader is warned however against expecting too much literal truth. Dominic's portrait has some of Guy Langton's features superimposed upon it: he understands Dominic's streak of violence because he is aware of its latent existence in himself. And throughout his life, Boyd himself experienced, as the fictional Dominic (if not the real Merric) is shown to have done, that feeling of never quite belonging to any group of which he was a member. The only good he recalled about being in the army as an officer was that, for a time, this feeling ceased to trouble him.

From this circumstance arose a recurrent theme of the novels, certainly of *Lucinda Brayford*, which meant most to him: the fruitless search by a woman, or sometimes a man, for a supreme attachment, to one who will accept simply and unconditionally a love and a fidelity which is offered in all innocence, without reserve. The story of Dominic and Helena might seem to contradict this statement. But the last sentence of *When Blackbirds Sing* casts a shadow over assurance. The fate of Dominic, hinted at in the beginning of *The Cardboard Crown* was evidently to be a tragic one, and it is not hard to guess what would have been the greatest tragedy for him. Boyd had intended to complete his story in a fifth novel, but tells us he refused to do so because his publishers wanted him to inject some sex and violence into the book. It may be so, but there is always the possibility that his own deeply concealed internal loneliness might have made it too painful for him to write, though he made several attempts; the later 1960s were not the happiest time for him emotionally.

The first of the Langton novels, *The Cardboard Crown*, introduces us to two of the elders of the tribe by whom Boyd was most influenced as a child, his grandfather, barrister and member of the Legislative Council, William Callander à Beckett, the 'Austin' of the novel, and his wife Emma Mills, the model for 'Alice'. William à Beckett was an extraordinarily able and versatile man, who served his state and his district diligently without finding sufficient outlet for all his energies. These erupted at times into eccentricities, though not of the long-drawn out kind attributed to him in the novel. Emma Mills brought great wealth into the family, made by her father's investments in breweries! There was also the suggestion of a convict taint, the result of a misunderstanding, but the story remained a well-kept secret until recently. Emma's wedding seems to have been the occasion of some drama, but whatever the circumstances of her married life, she, like her fictional counterpart, Alice, was a woman of great beauty and distinction, who was evidently the main-stay of the whole clan. One hopes fate dealt with her more kindly than with Alice. The book paints in, deftly and succinctly, the background to the family history, makes sense of the Langtons' divided loyalties, which caused them, like so many of their generation, to shuttle backwards and forwards between England and Australia, at home in both hemispheres. From the revised version of the book, the possibility that the sins of the fathers are visited on their children is ruled out, but the operation of malign influences from both past and present, working together with chance to shape destinies, remains a hypothesis. And never far below the brilliant surface of social life, even in the richest comic scenes are we allowed to forget the growing pressure of a mystery: the impossibility of defining and separating out what is good and what is evil from the warp and woof of existence, without the fabric falling apart.

In *A Difficult Young Man*, Dominic emerges from the background, a figure which the previous book prepares us to accept. He is after all the grandson of Austin and Alice, no slaves to convention. He is a moody, but handsome and attractive young man, whose best impulses are always doomed to be misunderstood and whose old-fashioned code of chivalry is so at odds with the new manners of his times as to be unrecognizable, even by those supposed to be of his own class. Moreover, his parents, Steven and Laura, are both artists, and have solved the problem of having insufficient money to keep up their social position by opting out of class altogether. They spend a short period of time, for Dominic's sake, at their ancestral home in Wiltshire, but, disgusted with English snobbery and distressed by the poverty of the villagers, they are glad to get back to Yarra Glen, their farm and their 'picnic' way of life. His parents' solution satisfies Dominic's brother Guy only intermittently; his head is full of Anglo-Catholic liturgies and medieval history, but his experience later teaches him the wisdom of their choice. In this second book, the conflict between commercialism and things that are valued in and for themselves becomes more overt and is embodied in the parabolic conflict between Dominic and his Aunt Baba, the worst type of social climber.

*Outbreak of Love* is perhaps the most misunderstood of the four novels. It is usually taken to be a frivolous interlude between the second and the fourth, and the dreadful irony of the title is ignored. The book is certainly full of extremely comic scenes, but under all of them, and under the book as a whole runs a current of unease which bears us inevitably to the 'outbreak' of war. It is a book full of little understated conflicts, between the 'Roman' and the 'provincial', the 'Teutonic' and the 'southern', none of which has anything to do with geography; between the heart and the head. Its account of the ease and swiftness with which war hysteria can be whipped up among supposedly civilized people, we have seen paralleled in recent times. The novel is usually referred to as a comedy of manners; a more accurate description would be 'a tragedy of manners'. As a study of the conflict between self-interest and self-transcendence, of the difference between smartness and good breeding, of the humanity that is the basis of all true courtesy, it could hardly be surpassed. The mediating consciousness of the book is chiefly Guy's, whose growth in compassion and understanding is one of its strengths. Among the most unforgettable scenes is the young man's sudden, almost physical awareness, after enjoying himself at a ball, of the agonizing loneliness of the unloved and the unlovable, in this case, of his ageing spinster aunt, against whom he has just been railing.

As in all the novels there are brief exquisite sketches of the Australian countryside, full of keen perceptiveness of its aloof aristocratic quality, its affinity with the archaic landscapes of Greece or Tuscany; there are no fake nymphs and satyrs here.

*When Blackbirds Sing* concentrates wholly on Dominic, using an omniscient narrator. It is concerned only with his war experience and the difference which this makes to the way he perceives himself in relation to the world. It is an entirely personal response, stated in a plain, direct style, which makes it all the more convincing. There is no attempt to argue that Dominic's attitude of mind has universal validity. It is himself he must finally answer to; there must be no more denial of his 'essential self', at someone else's bidding. By reason of its very simplicity the novel remains one of the most powerful arguments in Australian literature for the recognition of the common humanity of peoples.

This belief in the common humanity of peoples, 'the human godhead', is inseparable from Martin Boyd's religion. Men cannot function, he believed, without 'a necessary Myth' suited to their particular nature. For him, this was the Greco-Christian tradition wherein the pagan gods were redeemed in Christ. The literal truth did not bother him; the poetic truth was essential, though he objected to intellectuals who sprayed the literal truth 'with weed-killer' to cure simple people of superstition. In *A Single Flame* he subjects to rigorous scrutiny the simple faith taught him by his mother and his headmaster, Canon Long, of Trinity Grammar School and admits that it had no chance of surviving in the post-war world. But he distils from it a bedrock ethic acceptable to agnostics, which he calls 'the classical morality', and applies it to the situation of Europe in 1939. It is one of the finest statements of belief and of a basis for action of the period, and has lost none of its cogency. Theologically, its argument is that humankind is the Mystical Body of Christ and that therefore the brotherhood of man is a biological fact. Our neighbour, that is, is in a very real sense our self. There is much about Boyd's theology which reminds us of Karl Barth's, though in spite of his early theological training at St John's, Melbourne, Boyd had little use for professional theologians. The second important point he makes is to link politics and morality. He said once there were no political problems, only moral ones: 'If politicians had any morals, they wouldn't have any problems.' The statement remains true. So does the statement he made about Churchill's extravagant military gestures: 'No responsible man creates a chaos greater than his capacity to restore order.'

Boyd made a second attempt in England to lead an active religious life by joining a Franciscan order, but made the same mistake of expecting the gospels to be taken seriously. It was not until he was living near Cambridge during the second war, that his religion became again for him a vivid reality. This was partly due to the proximity of King's College Chapel, where he heard the finest music every day, but also to his friendship with Hugh l'Anson Fausset, a writer of unusual mind and spirit. He became a major influence on Boyd's thinking as a re-reading of his own books makes clear. He had a wide-ranging knowledge of European literature, as well as of religions other than Christianity. Like many writers, Boyd absorbed much of the information he needed from listening to the conversation of experts in their field, and he was fortunate in his friends. He disliked academics, and refused to think of himself as a 'man of letters'. To him, living was more important than writing, and people than places.

His boyhood home at Yarra Glen, his 'heart's home', remained for him the touchstone of his happiness, but his attempt to settle permanently in Australia in 1948, was unsuccessful. To escape the English winter, he finally settled in Rome, partly because of personal ties. These brought him no lasting happiness. He had however many good friendships to sustain him and an unwavering faith. The last energies of his writing life he spent writing a pamphlet defending youth and attacking the war-mongers who had dragged us into Vietnam.

As an expatriate, Boyd was accused more than once of 'rootlessness', a curious accusation to make against a writer whose bias is so obviously in favour of Australia. He replied that he was an expatriate more by accident than design, and that in any case his roots were within himself. He had learned that the search for an abiding city on earth is useless, and that where there are two or three kindred souls, there one can be at home.

An early reviewer once alluded to the 'quiet ferocity' of Boyd's style, a shrewd remark. He directed it as much against himself as his other targets: his books contain a number of satiric portraits of himself, some of which encourage the belief that he belonged among the aesthetes of the 1890s. There is no doubt about his passion for the beautiful, but not beauty at any price. For him, the good and the beautiful were indistinguishable, no more to be separated than God and Nature. It can be said of him that he used his art in their service, light-heartedly, at least on the surface, in an effort to awaken the sleeping to the presence within them of an essential self they had lost touch with. For that reason, he can at least be regarded as an honourable foot-soldier in the company in which Tolstoy and William Morris are leaders, leaders from whom Boyd learned some of his trade. All three saw through the shams and hypocrisies of their age with a peculiarly child-like clarity and an unanswerable logic, based on an unshakable conviction: 'In thee, O Good, have I put my trust.' Boyd wore his faith lightly, and frequently treated it in comic vein. There is no better guarantee of its firmness.

Dorothy Green

... death on the earth, in the sea, in the air —
Yet oh, it is a single soul always in the midst.

LAURENCE BINYON

... each is a single soul, a human being of feeling,
with ties of love and affection binding him to other
human beings. And each human being, each single soul
is a miracle, a forever incomprehensible mystery, a
fragment of the vast mystery of life itself.

DALLAS KENMARE *The Nature of Genius*

# CHAPTER ONE

ALL THE WAY HOME ON THE SHIP DOMINIC THOUGHT
of Helena. For the first week he had not so much thought
of her as felt her, or felt the loss of her. It was as if part of his
body had been torn off, and his life was pouring out of the
wound. He had so often been unhappy; though for brief
periods, an afternoon or a day when on a horse or in a boat,
the rhythm of riding or sailing had brought him into harmony with his surroundings, and he had felt an intense joy
of living, which, while it lasted, enabled him to forget his

[5]

inability to make any real contact with his fellows. When he tried to make it, he generally did something that infuriated them. At last, when he married Helena this obsession had left him; though his marriage had infuriated everybody, especially the way he did it, carrying her off while another man was waiting for her at the altar steps. Since then he had experienced nearly four years of at first bewildering happiness, which soon he came to regard as normal existence. His deep feeling for the natural world and his longing for complete human fellowship were satisfied on the farm where they lived in New South Wales.

And now he was separated from her for no one knew how long. It might be for ever if he were killed, for he was on his way to the war. He had very simple ideas of honour, as had Helena. If he had not gone to the war they might not have continued to be happy, knowing that their honour stood rooted in dishonour. Also Dominic had originally been intended for the army, but he had failed in his examinations, and he thought that now he had the opportunity to remedy this disgrace, which had overwhelmed him at the time. Again, with his inability to achieve a balanced relationship, either with people or between different facts, he did not realize, not in its full sharp meaning, what separation from his wife would involve.

In the anguish of this first week on the ship he was back again, a misfit new boy at school. It was partly to avoid these sensations that he was going home to join an English regiment, not so much from his own choice as on his father's advice. He had been going to enlist in the Australian Light Horse, but Steven had pointed out that Dominic's peculiar temperament, judging by his experience at school and at an agricultural college, appeared to arouse more hostility, or at any rate brutal ridicule, in the young Australian than in the young Englishman. So here he was on the ship, feeling again like the new boy; and ships in those days were very like small public schools. Committees were formed to organize games, and the members came round like prefects, forcing passengers to play. Cricket was almost compulsory for the men, and those crossing the line for the first time were forced to undergo the rites of Neptune.

It was very rough in the Great Australian Bight, and the public school spirit did not take control until the ship left Fremantle, so that for the first week Dominic was left alone in a deathly anguish which was almost physical. When he awoke in the night, and turned to touch the source of his life and peace, she was not there. She was hundreds of miles from him, and every hour the heaving ship took him further away. Not till then did he know how much she had given him. She had kept him serene, contained within himself, other than her, yet one with her in perfect harmony. He had lost all that tortured longing to escape his loneliness by meeting another person in the intimacy of anger. When he awoke in the morning and put his lips on her neck, her skin was full of cool, peaceful life. It was like dew. And she did not give him only physical peace. She calmed his mind. When, in spite of his general happiness, at times he thought that she did not really understand him and he felt his old impulse towards violent anger, which he had been told was an inherited taint in his blood, she did not meet it in any way, either in fear or repulsion, and it left him.

In the mornings he came into the saloon with his dark El Greco face looking haggard. A man at his table chaffed him about sea-sickness. Dominic did not answer. The man was one of that vast mass of people outside his comprehension, from whom formerly he had suffered so much in trying to win their friendship.

This was the first stage of the voyage when the other passengers either thought that he was seasick or were themselves too sick to notice him. In this stage he did not think, but only felt. He felt the loss of the integrity that Helena had given him, felt himself disintegrating, turning back into the bewildered perennial new boy.

The second stage began after Fremantle when the sports committee began to function. The sea was calm and he sat in his chair thinking of Helena. His feeling had become numbed with its own intensity and only gave him intermittent pangs. He filled his mind with pictures of her, in the dairy skimming the cream, or doing things with plums and apricots and tomatoes, drying them in the sun to use in the winter, or shaking the seeds from the pods of poppies. She was always engaged in country activities of this kind. Sometimes she was waiting for him, leaning over the gate when he came in from riding, or even sitting on the flat top of the gate post, which made him laugh. She also did this for him. He did not laugh easily and she released his laughter. He thought of her after their baby was born. He remembered his emotion, how through this she had brought him into the human fellowship from which he had always felt excluded, and had related him to the natural world which was his home.

One of the men organizing the games came up to him and told him that he was putting him down for the eleven against the ship's officers. Dominic said that he did not play cricket. The man laughed and said: "You can't get out of it with that one."

This was one of his difficulties in life. People so often could not believe the simplest facts when he told them. It was true that owing to his somewhat erratic education he had played hardly any cricket, and he did not like a game that was a sort of moral commitment and was even a substitute for a moral code. He thought games should be entirely for pleasure. He was not unathletic. He could break-in a colt and jump a five-barred gate. He was a strong swimmer and had dodged bulls in the arena at Arles.

He explained politely to the man that he saw no need to get out of it. The man gave him a curious look and after that left him alone. He explained to his committee that Dominic was a queer fish. Because of his dark, slightly foreign appearance, one of the passengers suggested that he might be a German spy. A Mrs Heseltine from Melbourne said that was nonsense, and that she knew his family quite well. She admitted that he was a bit of a black sheep, chiefly because he had run off with his first cousin, the bride of Wentworth McLeish, one of the richest squatters in the Western District, on the very day of the wedding.

Seeing him so lonely, and also attracted by his looks, she made herself known to him. He was longing for something or somebody familiar and he was always responsive to kindness and never questioned its sincerity. The numbness which succeeded his anguish was beginning to thaw. This friendly, pretty, rather frizzy woman who knew Aunt Mildred, though she was eighteen years older than himself, sent a warmth along his veins. For the first time since he left, his sombre face suddenly lighted up in a smile. He brought her deck chair and put it beside his own and they sat together for the rest of the voyage, the subject of a good deal of half-amused, half-malicious gossip.

They went ashore together at Durban, where he refused to go in a rickshaw, saying that he did not like being pulled by a human being.

"I must be able to say that I've ridden in one," she protested as she looked at a magnificent rickshaw boy, dressed in feathers, wearing huge horns, grinning and prancing and

*1                                                                    [9]

pretending to be a horse. But she allowed herself to be over-persuaded, not entirely disliking the sensation. Also she rather admired Dominic for refusing. She felt somehow that the same kind of hot pulsing blood beat in his veins as was in the African's. Dominic also felt this, but not so consciously, though it was indeed the reason why he would not have the African's noble body used as an animal's. As they walked in search of a cab, this feeling of affinity with the negro, whose impulses were not intellectualized, came up to his conscious mind, and produced a slight smouldering in him, that the man's splendid body should be exploited.

After two days ashore, seeing new things together, enjoying themselves and having a few slight arguments, they felt that they were old friends, and back on the ship their conversation became more intimate.

She asked him about his wife, and he told her how Helena had stayed to run the farm. It would have been too expensive for them all to come to England. The sea was calm from Cape Town to Teneriffe, and as the steamer crawled up through the warm drowsy ocean along the coast of Africa, he gradually unfolded to her the whole story of his life, in a way in which he had never confided to anyone else – not even to his mother, whom he could exasperate, nor to Helena for whom his confidence did not need words.

Mrs Heseltine had lost her husband in the previous year and was now on her way home to visit a young married daughter who lived at Wimbledon. When he told her how dreadful it had been leaving Helena she could understand, and there was a further bond between them. In this curiously unreal setting, he seemed for the first time to see himself and his life objectively. If he told her of some misfortune or disgrace that had come on him out of the blue, she showed him what it was in himself that had brought it about.

At Teneriffe she saved him from a scrape, but before it happened. They stood at the side of the ship, watching the local young men dive for coins thrown by the passengers. The water was an opalescent blue, but clear as glass, more vivid than he had ever seen it, even in the Pacific. The bodies of the young men were a golden brown, and as they fell like arrows into the sea, and moved about in marvellous patterns deep down in the opal clarity, Dominic's eyes glowed and darkened, as always when he saw something supremely beautiful, above all when it showed the freedom of men in the natural world.

"I want to do that," he said. "I'll go and change."

She put a hand on his arm and said: "No, you can't possibly."

"Why not? I'm a jolly good diver."

"You're an English gentleman. You can't dive for coins with natives."

"I'm an Australian: and they're not natives. They're Spaniards, so am I, partly."

"The captain would be furious."

"But it wouldn't hurt anyone," said Dominic, mystified.

"It wouldn't be dignified."

He could not see what she meant. It was as if she had said that a tiger, its stripes spotted with sunlight as it moved through jungle shadows, or swallows whirling in the autumn sky, were not dignified. The divers moving in patterns beneath the translucent sea were not only beautiful to watch; he also thought that they must feel the water as a fish feels it, and savour its acrid salts as a fish would do. Was a man standing a few yards away, his body misshapen from a sedentary life and clad in hot brown tweeds, more dignified?

Mrs Heseltine laughed at Dominic's inability to understand the values of this world. He mentioned these divers two or three times before they parted, and they argued about the meaning of dignity.

Between Teneriffe and Plymouth they were in the submarine area. In the evening the decks were darkened and some of the men did not change, feeling vaguely that it would show a lack of seriousness to be drowned in a dinner jacket. Dominic did not have this sense of propriety, and his white shirt gleamed faintly where he sat in his deck chair beside Mrs Heseltine, advertising their association till the last moment.

In the darkness and the danger their conversation became more intimate, about the needs of the body and the soul. At times he surprised her by the simplicity of his wants and his aims. At other times she felt that he was asking for the whole world. He treated her more as a confidante than as a woman whom he might desire. She was glad that the voyage was ending, as in spite of the difference in their ages, she felt that she would soon be preposterously in love with him. On the last evening before they arrived at Plymouth, he said goodnight to her in the narrow corridor outside her cabin.

"Well," she said, "I suppose this is almost goodbye." She allowed her semi-maternal love for him to show in her eyes. He was used to this look in women's eyes, but unless it was a woman towards whom he felt a strong physical attraction, he only responded to it with a kind of boyish friendliness. He looked at her now with affection and gratitude.

"Without you the voyage would have been unbearable," he said.

They shook hands, and she did not let his go. Not quite knowing what to do, he kissed it. She then said goodnight again and turned into her cabin.

"Really, he's a little silly," she thought.

Dominic walked slowly to his cabin. He was sorry that they had to part, and he thought that he owed her a great deal. She had eased the wretchedness of his separation from Helena by allowing him to talk about it. Helena was no longer a torn-off part of his body, with his life pouring out through the wound. She was what he most desired, but he was once more a complete being in himself, and Mrs. Heseltine had done this for him. She had in some odd way given him back his integrity.

He thought that it would be nice to see her sometimes in London, and to renew their talks. They had already exchanged addresses. But it turned out that she had fulfilled her one function in his life, and when he remembered this voyage, the Spanish divers were more vivid in his mind.

## CHAPTER TWO

MOST OF THE PASSENGERS LEFT THE SHIP AT Plymouth and went to London by train; partly because they were tired of the long voyage, but more because, having escaped the submarines, they thought it would be foolish to take a further and greater chance of being drowned, or of floating about the Channel in lifebelts. They were all ashamed of giving these very sensible reasons and made up excuses about appointments in London.

Dominic disembarked at Plymouth because his father had asked him to look in at Waterpark, the ancient inherited home of their family, in which, for the past two generations, they had made repeated nostalgic attempts to live, always ending in a sudden flight back to the sunlight and freedom of Australia. These were sometimes due to loss of money, but the occasion of the last flight, about five years earlier, was the rather discreditable way in which Dominic had provoked the breaking of his engagement to Sylvia Tunstall, the daughter of their nearest neighbours, the Diltons. He was now supposed to see how much the tenant's continual demands for repairs were justified. Mrs Heseltine, who had little money and a cheerful fatalistic attitude to danger, went on in the ship.

When Dominic left the train at Frome, the once familiar station seemed strange to him. It was all dreamlike, as if the air were less dense, or the law of gravity modified. There was a new station-master who did not know him. When he told him his name, recently so well known in the county, he showed no sign of recognition, but he told him where he could hire a motor-car to drive out to Waterpark, seven miles away. The driver of the car knew who he was, but did not give him any effusive welcome to his home town. Dominic felt lonely and flat. As they drove along the deep lanes the sense of being isolated and alien to his own countryside grew stronger. It occurred to him, too late, that when he arrived at Waterpark in a car piled with his luggage, he would not necessarily be made welcome by Mr Cecil, the tenant, whom he had never met. He had followed the long habit of his youth and, without thinking, had put his luggage in the car at Frome station. As a small child he had been met there by one of his grandfather's carriages, and as a young man by his father's motor-car. He felt one of those curious stoppages in his brain, which happened when he suddenly found that he had acted instinctively without regard to changed circumstances. For a moment he could not think what to do. He was just going to tell the man to turn back. He would stay at the inn at Frome and come out again the next day. The man would think him mad, as people often did when to his own mind he acted sensibly.

Just then he saw the Dilton gates ahead of him, with the two stone greyhounds on the pillars. He told the driver to turn in. He did not doubt that the Tunstalls would welcome him, though he had not seen them for five years, and their last meeting, when he had practically jilted Sylvia, had been the most awkward possible. He judged other people by himself, and as he never nursed a grievance, he was sure that they would welcome him with the same affection, which, remembering only happy times, he felt as the car sped through the familiar park. He was sure that his arrival would be a pleasant surprise, and that with homely warmth, which had never been a Tunstall trait, he would immediately be restored to the family circle.

But when the car stopped below the steps of the huge late Georgian house there was little sign of welcome or even of life. The blinds were drawn in many rooms, and the front door had that indefinable look, perhaps from dust in the jambs, of being seldom opened.

Again he had the feeling of changed laws of gravity, and sometimes in later life he dreamed of this arrival at the forbidding door of Dilton, itself at this moment like something in a dream. But his feeling did not prevent him telling the driver to take out his luggage, and he paid him off. He rang, but it was a long time before the door was opened, and then not by the butler whom he knew, but by a parlourmaid. He asked if Miss Sylvia was at home.

"Miss Sylvia's been married two years," said the young

woman, looking with puzzled disapproval at this apparently foreign gentleman, and the luggage piled at the bottom of the steps.

"Is his lordship in?" asked Dominic.

"His lordship's at the depot."

"What depot?"

"Where he's the colonel," said the parlourmaid, slightly indignant at his ignorance.

"Oh." Dominic thought for a moment. He had asked for the family according to the degree of attachment he had had for them. He realized he should first have asked for Lady Dilton, and did so now. "Will you tell her Mr Langton's here?" he said.

She told him to wait, and she shut the heavy iron-studded door in his face. Like the people on the ship she thought that he might be a spy. In a few minutes he heard again the grating of the bolts and she reappeared, asking him to enter. Lady Dilton, her curiosity aroused by the parlourmaid, who had given his name wrongly, had come out into the vast empty hall. Dominic was standing against the light.

"Who is it?" she asked with the fretfulness of a large woman who is a little nervous.

"It's me, Dominic," he said.

"Oh!" She hesitated a moment, then added: "Come in." She led the way back into the little drawing-room which she used mostly during the war, and turned to face him.

"Well, this is a surprise," she said, without excessive geniality, but she shook hands. "I didn't know you were in England."

He explained that he had just arrived, that he had been going to Waterpark, but passing Dilton he had come in to see them.

[16]

"Where are you staying?" she asked.

"I don't know."

"Where is your luggage?"

"On the steps."

She smiled with that grim smile which Dominic had sometimes provoked in her. When she had seen him in the hall she had felt indignation which had lain dormant since their last encounter. But it had only been a flicker, and now it died.

"You'd better stay here," she said. "That parlourmaid's a fool. All the men have gone into the army." She tugged a bell pull and when the maid came she told her to take the luggage up into Mr Richard's room. She explained that both her sons were in France.

"I suppose you have come over to fight for us," she said. This made her more inclined to let bygones be bygones.

"Yes," said Dominic, though it had not occurred to him that he had come over to fight for Lady Dilton. He thought that he had come so that he and Helena, or if he did not return, Helena and the baby, could go on living on their farm in New South Wales, and so that it would not be a German colony.

"Sylvia's married?" he said.

"Yes, to Maurice Wesley-Maude."

"Is he nice?"

Again Lady Dilton gave her grim smile. "He's a gentleman," she admitted. "I heard you are married too."

"Yes, to Helena Craig."

"Well, that's a good thing." Lady Dilton was uninterested in the identity of Dominic's wife, but apparently felt that it made things easier now that both he and Sylvia were safely tied up elsewhere. They talked for a while about what had happened in their families since they last met. He asked about the tenants at Waterpark.

"We don't know them very well," she said. "They don't shoot. I think the man reads books."

Colonel Rodgers, her brother, who rented the dower-house at Waterpark, and who had tried, at the cost of much suffering, to found with Dominic, in his adolescence, a friendship based on a mutual passion for lethal weapons, was in London angling for a job in the War Office. She gave him the address of his club, and told him to be sure and go to see him. Sylvia had a tiny house behind Buckingham Gate. "They are very poor," she explained. Dominic knew that Sylvia had an allowance of a thousand a year, and her husband presumably had some money, if only his army pay. "The house is no bigger than a box," she went on. "Sylvia says it is smart. That is not a word we used in my younger days. Only vulgar people were smart." She did not give him Sylvia's address, and it was obvious that she thought it better not. All Lady Dilton's subtleties and snubs were obvious. Anyone who cared to point this out could have brought about a collapse of her immense dignity, but most people whom she met were too intimidated, and her friends of equal position were too kind, or else behaved in the same way themselves.

At last she said: "I must get on with these wretched circulars. Perhaps you would help me?" For the first time in her life when she needed a secretary, she had not got one.

She gave him a list of names and addresses, and they sat down at opposite sides of a large regency writing-table, contentedly scribbling away. Sometimes she spoke to him rather crossly, saying that his writing was illegible, and that he ought to leave more space for the stamps. The intimacy of this made him contented. The awful isolation he had felt at times on the ship, in spite of Mrs Heseltine, had left him. Here he was in a house he knew, within an hour, back as one of the family, being scolded for his untidy writing. This was what he liked best, to be at ease in familiar places with people who knew him well, who knew the worst things he had done but had accepted them. Also in this house he had known hours of blissful happiness in the days when he was engaged to Sylvia.

They were interrupted by the entry of Lord Dilton in khaki. He looked surprised, and waited for his wife to explain and introduce the young man sitting opposite her at the table. Then he saw that it was Dominic, and as in his wife five years' resentment awoke, flickered and died.

"Good God, Dominic!" he exclaimed, and shook hands warmly.

"He has come over to fight for us," said Lady Dilton, thinking this might temper her husband's possible annoyance, but he appeared delighted to see Dominic. He chatted for a few moments and then said: "I hope to goodness the water's hot tonight. I'm afraid that you'll be confoundedly uncomfortable here. We've no men and the monstrous regiment of women can't stoke the boiler. Have they lit a fire in Dominic's room? And is there one in mine?"

"We weren't certain that you were coming," said Lady Dilton.

"It's better for me to have pneumonia than to waste sixpence worth of coal," he said to Dominic. He only went on like this when he was in high spirits.

"It's not the coal," said his wife. "They get bad-tempered if they have to light a fire for nothing."

"Is there a fire in Dominic's room?"

"I don't know."

"If the depot was run like this house we'd soon lose the war," he said.

They argued a little more as to where Dominic should

have his bath, and finally agreed that the water in the green bathroom was generally hotter as it was nearer the boiler. Lady Dilton again pulled the bell rope and Dominic felt that the whole of the enormous house was buzzing with preparations for his bath. Lord Dilton said: "I must go down and find something for you to drink."

Dominic lay in his bath in a state of contented relaxation of mind and body. This was the first freshwater bath he had had for over six weeks, since he left Melbourne. He disliked the smell of hot salt water, and here not only was the water fresh, but the soap had a delicious scent of aromatic leaves. He was glad that he had found the Diltons alone. He might have been embarrassed at meeting Sylvia, though he wanted to see her. The boys, now smart young guardees, might have made him feel too much a back-woodsman. The house itself was more friendly, with its slight domestic incompetence, than with its former grandeur.

He wondered if Sylvia had ever used this bath. He thought that she must have; in spite of the size of the house, there were few bathrooms, and they were converted bedrooms. He wondered what it would have been like to have married her. If he had, they would now have been living in the dower-house at Waterpark, having turned out Colonel Rodgers. Perhaps she had used this bath. She had a lovely skin, and he thought with her golden hair against the pale green enamel she must have looked wonderfully beautiful. Back in this house, with the Diltons so kind, the atmosphere of those days was returning to him. He felt that he had missed something that should have been his.

He lay so long in the bath that he came down only a few moments before dinner was announced. Lady Dilton looked a little forbidding, as she thought that he was going to be late; but when he said: "The water was so hot that I couldn't get out of the bath," she glanced at him almost with affection.

They dined at a small table, a pool of light in the dim spaces of the dining-room, which increased the feeling of family intimacy. Lord Dilton had brought up a very special burgundy, which he and Dominic finished between them, as his wife drank only whisky. He asked Dominic what regiment he was going to join, and said that if he would like to get a commission in the territorials of which he was the colonel, he would be pleased to ask for him. They drafted their officers and men to the regular battalion in France when they were ready. "But perhaps you want something less humdrum?" he suggested. "Cavalry, eh? Their turn will come."

Dominic said that his father had advised him to apply to the colonel of his grandfather Byngham's regiment, so that he would not be quite unknown.

"I suppose you should do what your father wants," said Lord Dilton. "But a Langton would not be unknown in a west country regiment."

When he left to return to the depot he again referred to this, and told Dominic that if he changed his mind he would be very glad to have him as a subaltern.

In the morning Dominic continued to help Lady Dilton with her circulars. In the afternoon she had to go to preside over a committee and he asked if he might have some means of transport, a horse or a motor-car or a bicycle to go over to Waterpark. Only a bicycle was available, and he set out along the country lanes, through which he had so often ridden when he was in love with Sylvia.

He no longer had the feeling of yesterday, that the local air was not his natural element. He was reacclimatized. For him it was not true that the skies but not the soul had changed. Under these English skies the emotions he felt here were stirring again. As he turned into the avenue, still with its notice: "Wheels to Waterpark House only," he captured for a moment something of the wild delight he felt when he rode back here, also on a bicycle, to announce his engagement to Sylvia.

Dominic was still adolescent in the sense that he retained the vivid perceptions of childhood. He was as excited by the Spaniards moving in golden patterns beneath the water as a child would have been. He had not, like so many boys with a more conventional education, had his ideas of "manliness" and his limits of allowable perception fixed at the age of fifteen. He was not one of the permanent or petrified adolescents, who have come absolutely to terms with the surface of life; and who call themselves, with perhaps a regret for that lost glimpse of a greater reality, "old boys" until life itself is ended. He continued experimenting, emotional, searching for some kind of truth which he felt that everyone else possessed and which was the secret of happiness. So he remained adolescent, which at least gave him the chance of reaching a complete, and not merely an external, maturity.

He left his bicycle against the high stone wall which separated the garden from the avenue, and opened the wooden door in the wall, which curiously was the main entrance to the house.

He forgot the politeness due to the tenant, and he walked across the lawn to the bridge by the three oak trees. Beyond was the meadow path to the village, by which he had often gone to see Colonel Rodgers. Memories returned, disturbing him. He felt that he had missed something, had taken the wrong turning. It was late September. The morning had been misty, but now the sun had come through. In the long border against the wall were blooming michaelmas daisies, and the white Japanese anemones and the different kinds of yellow sunflowers which his mother used to arrange in such splendid bunches against the white and gold walls of the drawing-room. The chestnuts in the avenue were turning yellow, and across the meadow were golden patches in the elm trees around the church. The sunlight warmed the old bricks of the house, and there was absolute stillness, a tremendous sense of peace and of the peacefulness of the past, and he felt somehow that this peace was his natural element. He felt himself to be as much a part of this old place as the three oak trees by the stream, the bricks in the wall. He leaned on the bridge, looking down into the stream, and remembering how close its intimate life had seemed to him as a child. He was disturbed by a voice behind him asking sharply: "Do you want anything?"

He turned and saw Mr Cecil, the tenant, though he was as yet unaware of his identity.

"Oh, good afternoon," said Dominic. "I've come to see the house."

"And do you often come to see other people's houses?" asked Mr Cecil, with an air of amusement.

"Well, really it's my house, or rather my father's," Dominic explained.

"You are one of Mr. Langton's sons?"

"Yes, I've come to see about the repairs."

"Then you are very welcome."

Mr Cecil shook hands. He led the way across the lawn, and learning which of Steven's sons he was talking to, he told him that he had heard much about him from Colonel Rodgers, whom he described as "an engaging but reprehensible character".

He took Dominic from room to room, a door-handle was needed here; a piece of skirting broken there; and the mysterious patch of damp had appeared again on the staircase wall.

They ended up in the drawing-room where the white panelled walls, with their carved and gilded classical motifs were almost entirely covered with shelves full of books. The library shelves were also full of Mr Cecil's books, and he had taken the house because of that accommodation. The room had a comfortable academic appearance, but all its grace and richness of colour were gone. It was the same throughout the house. It had more the atmosphere of a kind of clergyhouse than of the home of people who were engaged in a full-blooded enjoyment of life.

Mr Cecil's conversation, when he had dealt with dilapidations, had a curious dry flavour that went with the appearance of the house. He mentioned the war, and said, as if it would be merely an interesting phenomenon: "We shall have a great recrudescence of violence when it is all over."

"But that is what we are fighting against," protested Dominic.

"You can kill men's bodies with guns, not their ideas," said Mr Cecil.

Dominic was bothered by this remark. The idea of pausing in the middle of a crusade to question its probable results was alien to him. He refused an invitation to stay to tea, saying that he wanted to see the church, and he had to return to Dilton before dark, as his bicycle had no lamp. He said goodbye, asking Mr Cecil to have the repairs done by a builder in Frome, as there was no longer an estate carpenter, and to send the bill to Steven.

As he wheeled his bicycle across the lawn, and took the meadow path to the church, he was a little depressed by the atmosphere of his former home. Whatever misfortunes had come on the family in this place, while they lived there it had always been a lively, friendly house. His depression was increased when he met a tall woman in grey tweeds and a man's hat, who stopped him and said: "Are you aware that you are trespassing?"

"No," said Dominic, surprised.

"How did you get on to this path?"

"I've been to see Mr Cecil at the house."

"Did he give you permission to come this way?"

"He didn't say I mustn't. Are you the new vicar's wife?"

"I am Mrs Cecil of Waterpark House."

Dominic thought of replying: "And I am Mr Langton of Waterpark House." Instead he explained politely: "I am just going to see the church."

"Why aren't you in uniform?" she asked.

"I've only just arrived in England."

She looked sceptical, said: "Don't dawdle," and nodded goodbye.

He was thankful that he had not arrived last night with all his luggage.

He had never much liked going to church, but now the place restored his sense of belonging here, weakened by his meeting with the Cecils. This was largely because of the names of his forebears on the tombs, and the more heraldic than religious stained glass which his grandfather had put in their chapel.

He browsed about the church, giving the names on the tombs more attention than he had done before when he was a boy and had taken them for granted. There were several Stevens. It was odd to see his father's name on these memorial plaques, and it increased his feeling of belonging. The roots of his family were here. The powerful influences of the place made him believe that it was impossible that they should live anywhere else.

He left the church and rode along the village street.

When he came to the dower-house, a small Elizabethan house in the village, although he knew that Colonel Rodgers was in London, he alighted from his bicycle and knocked at the low door, which was opened by Mrs Hawke, the Colonel's housekeeper. She gave him a questioning look and then exclaimed: "Master Dominic! This is a surprise!" She sounded as if it were a more welcome one than it had been to Lady Dilton. "Oh, the colonel will be upset to miss you! He's away in London looking for work. Come in and I'll give you some tea. I'd never hear the end of it if I didn't give you tea."

He stood again in the low dark-beamed sitting-room, the walls hung with the spears and swords, the battle pictures and the shrunken and mummified natives' heads on the mantelpiece. Nothing had changed except that between the mummified heads was a large photograph of himself at the age of eighteen. He felt a longing to recover the life in which he used to visit this house, to be an integral part of the community. He was moved by the photograph of himself, to know that for the years he had been away, in which he had hardly given Colonel Rodgers a thought, he had been remembered.

Mrs Hawke brought his tea. She stood and gossiped while he drank it, and ate her good cakes, the same kind that she had always made, the taste of which telescoped his absent years. The names of the village people of whom she gave him news were like the flavour of the cakes. Young Jonas was in the army. Miriam, the Wakes' girl had got into trouble, which Mrs Hawke put down to her going courting without a hat. She had gone to London, as usual leaving the baby with its grandparents. The old vicar was dead at last.

Dominic asked her about the Cecils.

"They!" she said contemptuously. "They do nothing for the village. You tell your father with proper respect he ought to come home again. Waterpark without Langtons isn't Waterpark, that's what I say."

When he left Mrs Hawke he was certain that they should all return to Waterpark. In this secluded village, where the medieval pattern had hardly changed, lay their secure identity. They had taken the wrong turning when they left it. He had not taken the wrong turning when he married Helena, but he should have brought her to live here. As he rode back to Dilton he was full of the idea of their return.

He dined alone with Lady Dilton and told her that he wanted the family to come back to live in their original home.

"That would be a good thing," she said approvingly.

She went to bed at ten o'clock. He sat up in his room, writing to Helena a long letter explaining how, after the war, they must all return to live at Waterpark, his parents at the house, themselves at a farm near by, as long as Colonel Rodgers was alive.

This was the first real letter he had written to her. In the weeks immediately following their separation, his misery had been so great that he could find no words to express it. He had only sent a note from Durban, and another from Cape Town, saying that it was a dull voyage and sending her all his love. Now this, his first real letter was full, not with longing for the scenes of their home, but of plans for her own transportation. And he was staying at Dilton, and he did not tell her that Sylvia, to whom he had been engaged, was married and living in London.

He also wrote to his father, advocating a new migration. Steven received this plan with little enthusiasm, but he was amused at Dominic's staying at Dilton. It was the last thing he would have expected, and therefore he should have foreseen it, as Dominic always did the last thing one would expect.

## CHAPTER THREE

DOMINIC LEFT DILTON THE NEXT DAY AND ARRIVED in London in the evening. On Paddington station they were lifting wounded soldiers into a train at the next platform. He stood watching them, as a child will sometimes stand, absolutely still and expressionless, fixedly looking at something which it has never seen before, storing it at the back of its mind. The porter interrupted him by asking what he should do with his luggage, and he told him to take it into the station hotel, where he spent the night.

In the morning he went to his bank in Threadneedle Street to collect his letters. There were about a dozen, nearly all from relatives in Australia. Two of them were from Helena, one from his mother, in which she told him not to forget to go to see old Cousin Emma, and one from Cousin Emma herself inviting him.

He sat on a mahogany chair in the bank and opened Helena's letters. The first which he read was dated about ten days after he left. It described in detail their life on the farm, and the antics of the baby. He read it more with concentrated interest than with emotion. If he had received it at Fremantle in the first stages of his voyage, every word would have given a twinge to his longing to be home. Now he was full of his plans to bring them back to Waterpark, and Helena's aim in writing in this way, to keep vividly before him the picture of his home, was without a target. When she received his letter written from Dilton she was dismayed. Her other letter was written on the evening he had left. He read:

> *My darling Dominic,*
>
> *I don't know how I am going to live without you. I cannot bear to think how long it may be till you come back. Now it seems that you have just gone to Sydney and will be back tomorrow. I can't believe any-thing else. I shall only be able to live by thinking all the time that you will be back tomorrow and then one day it will be true. I cannot write to you how much I love you. I do not know the language. I am not good at writing what I feel. I am afraid that you are not, either. So all the time we must simply remember each other in our hearts. Our letters will only help us a little. But I love you.*
>
> > *Helena.*

He sat for a long time holding this letter. A yard or two away men came in and cashed their cheques or paid in others. One or two glanced at him curiously, thinking that he must have heard some dreadful news. Some of the anguish of his first week on the ship returned to him, and from this letter he received the vivid impression of his home life, which her detailed description had not brought him. He read the other letters in the bus going back to Paddington, but he did not take in their contents.

In the afternoon he walked across Kensington Gardens to Brompton Square to see Cousin Emma, not only as a duty, but because his father had said that she might be useful to him. She seemed to know all the generals, as her husband, nicknamed Coco, had been in the War Office, and had helped some of the most famous in their careers. She even referred to Lord Kitchener as "one of Coco's boys".

Like the Diltons, she apppeared to have buried the hatchet, as Dominic had lodged with her while he attended a crammer's, and their parting had been far from cordial. One of his few good fortunes was that people thought well of him in his absence. They remembered his good looks, his genuine desire for friendship, and his suggestion of smouldering passion, which was particularly attractive to women.

She looked at him critically and thought that he had become rather colonial. After a few enquiries about his parents and, as an afterthought, his wife and child, telling him that one of the latter was enough, she put him through a sort of catechism. She asked where he was staying, and told him that he could not go on living at a station hotel on the wrong side of the park. She gave him the address of a small inexpensive hotel off Curzon Street, where "people of our sort" could stay. But her chief concern was the most socially desirable way in which he could serve his country.

He told her that he intended to join the regiment in which so many of the Bynghams, his mother's family, had served. She thought that a good idea, as he would begin with some background. He said too that Lord Dilton had asked him to join the territorial battalion of the local regiment, of which he was colonel. She was impresssed by Lord Dilton's wanting Dominic, but she had been so involved in the life of the regular army that she considered being a territorial to be almost degrading. She told him to go to see another distant relative, a colonel in the War Office.

When he left her, he took a bus to Piccadilly, and walked down St James's Street to call on Colonel Rodgers at his club. The colonel was in. His strange angry eyes glittered with excitement at seeing Dominic. He gripped his hand and led him upstairs into an empty card-room. "This is great! This is great! Thank God you've come!" he repeated. He had been afraid that Dominic was not coming to the war. If he had not arrived soon he would have removed his photograph from between the mummified heads.

"Why didn't you come before?" he asked. Dominic explained that he could not leave until Helena's baby was born, and she was able to manage the farm in his absence.

"A soldier can't consider that sort of thing," said the colonel. "Well, these are splendid times, splendid times!" he went on when they were seated in leather armchairs. "The greatest war in history! I'm too old to fight in it, but thank God I'm alive to see it. I'm after a job in the War Office. It should come through soon." He talked of the conduct of the war, criticizing much of it from the angle of his experiences amongst the Zulus and the Boers and the Afghans. He abused Mr Asquith violently, and repeated atrocious slanders about his family. He was so sure that he was an English gentleman, that even if he spread the vilest rumours, automatically that became the correct thing to do.

Dominic was a little dazed when he left him. Lady Dilton thought he had come over to fight for her. Cousin Emma thought he had come over to improve his social position in a good regiment. The colonel thought he had come to provide the vicarious satisfaction of his fighting spirit. Dominic did not yet repudiate their respective attitudes. He was only bewildered.

The next day he moved to the little hotel in Mayfair

and then he went to see the other colonel, the relative in the War Office, an oldish man, recalled from retirement. He appeared very conscientious, and not much given to nepotism. He asked Dominic if he had any military experience, and when he answered no, suggested that he should join the Inns of Court O.T.C. for a period of training. He asked him a few questions about his father, and if he intended returning to Waterpark. He then said goodbye and hoped that he would like the army.

Dominic felt that it would be an anticlimax having come all this way to join a leisurely training corps of lawyers, who in that year still lived in their own homes, and paraded on the lawns of Lincoln's Inn. Instead he wrote to the colonel of the Byngham family's regiment, which was stationed in Northumberland. His handwriting was immature, and he expressed himself in simple, almost friendly terms, saying that he had had many relatives in the regiment, but not mentioning that their name was Byngham, nor that one of them had commanded the regiment at Waterloo, nor even that they had been commissioned officers.

The colonel of this regiment saw no reason to accept as one of his subalterns an unknown Australian who wrote to him in this strain; and Dominic had only an acknowledgement from the adjutant, saying that they were up to strength.

On receipt of this note, Dominic wrote to Lord Dilton saying that he would very much like to join the territorial battalion. As soon as he was commissioned he went down and reported at the depot.

It might have been thought that in the army Dominic would make appalling blunders and get into endless scrapes, but he took to the life immediately. He went through his training and was soon an efficient subaltern.

He enjoyed the intricacies of drill, and when told to, could move the battalion about with perfect confidence. He had a new happiness. At last he was doing the same kind of thing as other young men, doing it in their company and doing it well. For the first time in his life he had that kind of companionship, and was no longer an outsider.

Lord Dilton was delighted and talked of putting him on the establishment. He had asked Dominic to join the regiment partly from kindness, and partly because he liked to have officers of whom he knew. The other subalterns were either from local families, or were the sons of his friends.

Impulsively Dominic wrote to Helena, saying that he wanted to stay in the army after the war, and he repeated the suggestion that they should all return to Waterpark. With the half-conscious dishonesty of people trying to get their own way, he said that it would be a much more enjoyable life for her.

Helena had been quietly happy on the morning she received this letter. She had left the baby with the new fresh country girl she had found to help her in the house, and had ridden to the box two miles away, where the letters were left in a leather bag. There should be a letter from Dominic. Now, perhaps as a result of the discipline of military life, he wrote regularly once a week. It was a still winter day, the sunlight gentle and sparkling. The notes of the magpies and other sounds were music in the limpid air. She felt more hopeful than usual. Perhaps the war would be over before Dominic reached the front. Perhaps this time next year he would be back and they would be riding together for the post, but they would not care twopence whether there were any letters. She had been thinking out further improvements to the house and garden. She had begun on some of them, but what fun it would be when they were doing it again together. How wonderful their life would be. They were happy before, but they took it as a matter of course. When their happiness had been rescued from disaster, every minute would be wonderful. She could think of no better life than theirs, to live on their own land in this perfect climate, where nearly all the good food they ate was grown by themselves, where their human contacts were dictated by inclination and not social compulsion, and where all the time they were improving this beautiful natural setting as a home for their children. She loved all the life of the country, skimming the pans in the dairy, gathering the fruit for the year's jam from the orchard, most of which they had planted themselves and which was just beginning to bear. It seemed to her that they had all the enduring pleasures that were intended for mankind, and the only deep satisfactions, creative contentment in the natural world.

She arrived at the box, and taking a little key from her pocket, she opened the leather bag, finding as she had expected, Dominic's letter. She sat on her horse and read it, and the sparkling air seemed to become flat, and the light on the grass to go dead. She rode miserably home. In every letter that she had written to him she had described some part of the life of the farm, telling him even the number of bunches of grapes on the verandah vine; that the new cow had calved and how much milk it was giving; what new plants she had put in the garden. Everything she wrote was intended to keep the place vivid in his mind. Everything she did was for him and to make it ready for his return. It was the only way she could express her love. She was like the medieval tumbler whose only means of worship was to do his tricks before the image of the Virgin. Her parents and also Dominic's had offered her a home while he was away, where she could have lived without expense in idle comfort, but she would not give up this, the only way she had of serving him.

Now, suddenly, it had all become nothing. This home which was a kind of symbol of their love, was to be abandoned, and they were to live in a place which they had done nothing to make, in a country which, though it was partly Dominic's, was very little hers; or worse, in ever-changing lodgings among army wives.

She tried to explain this in a letter. When she had written it she thought it sounded complaining, and she had resolved, after that first short note, that she would always write cheerfully. But she was writing into a void. Dominic, though he now wrote regularly, conveyed to her nothing of his life. She heard indirectly of things he never mentioned. There were rumours from Melbourne of his behaviour on the ship. These things made her loyally angry. People seemed determined to speak ill of Dominic, however great the nonsense they talked. Aunt Baba wrote that he had behaved disgracefully, spending the voyage exclusively in the company of a fast woman twice his age, with whom he flirted outrageously; but Dominic had not mentioned any woman. He liked talking to older women because they understood him better. She was sure that this was the origin of the scandal, though she could not help feeling jealous of this unknown woman, of whom he had told her nothing. He had been at Dilton, and he had joined his regiment. He must have met Sylvia, but he did not say so. He only told her details of his army life, or put forward this horrible plan for their future. She felt like a mother whose son has gone to his first school. She knows that he is a sensitive child, brave but nervous, and she longs to know if it is as bad as he feared. She only receives a letter: "Dear Mum, Our second eleven beat Weldon's. Hawkins is the captain. I am learning geography. Your loving son. . . ."

Her only comfort was that Dominic had ended his letter: "All my love."

She wrote to Steven about the plan to return to Waterpark. He replied telling her not to worry, that nothing on earth would drag him back to English winters. Anyhow, they could not afford to live there. They could barely do so before. With the heavy taxation to pay for the war it would be impossible. She tore up her complaining letter and wrote again to Dominic saying that his father had told her that it was financially impossible. This saved her having to give her own reasons.

## CHAPTER FOUR

ONE DAY IN THE ANTE-ROOM DOMINIC NOTICED THAT the colonel was looking at him speculatively, as if trying to decide something. Then he crossed over to him and said: "Sylvia and her husband are down for a few days. Would you like to come back with me to dine tonight?"

Dominic said that he would very much like to come. He had not realized until that moment how much he wanted to see Sylvia. He thought it was largely curiosity, but he felt rather excited during the afternoon.

They arrived just before dinner and found the family

in the big drawing-room, which was opened up for the occasion. Apart from the women servants the house was still run more or less as in peace-time, and Lord Dilton's complaint of acute discomfort was only due to the alleged tepidity of the bath water, and his reluctance to give the keys of the cellar to a woman.

When they came in Sylvia turned sharply to look at Dominic. After his first visit her mother, seeing eye to eye with Cousin Emma, had written to her that he had become rather colonial and scrubby. She expected this evening to feel a mixture of friendly condescension and relief at what she had escaped. But a few months of army life had made a great difference to Dominic's appearance. It had brought out certain traits and attitudes which were latent in his blood. Lord Dilton generally changed when he was at home, but tonight he and Dominic were both in uniform. Dominic did not look at all scrubby. Women are said to like men in uniform, and it did give him a particular kind of aplomb, that sombre Spanish appearance, which when he was in ordinary clothes and holding himself more care- lessly, might pass for mere sulkiness. He had not the farouche romantic bloom of five years earlier, but as a man he was immensely improved. When Sylvia saw him she gave a little start of surprise, and perhaps faintly of mortification.

She herself was no longer the pretty petulant girl to whom he had been engaged. She had become a woman of the world, extremely *soignée*. She was one of those whose good taste and artistry function most successfully when concentrated on their own persons. Tonight, even in this splendid room with its great mirrors and gilded ceiling, she looked the living centre of golden light, in her dress of stiff flowered yellow silk. She still had the "rose-petal skin" so much talked of in her schooldays, but her golden hair looked less frizzy than then, and held richer and softer lights, while her features had now achieved an absolute classical perfection. When they shook hands they stared at each other, amazed at what they had missed.

"You haven't changed," she said. "Mother said you'd changed." She meant, not in the way that Lady Dilton had said.

She introduced her husband, Maurice Wesley-Maude. He was very much an army type, with a round red face, narrow blue eyes, clipped speech and a clipped moustache. He was a major in a regiment of hussars, where, Lady Dilton confided later and almost deprecatingly to Dominic, the officers were mostly the sons of rich manufacturers, though Maurice's father was a canon of Exeter. Again it seemed that the army's *raison d'être* was to assess social status.

After three unsuccessful London seasons Sylvia had accepted Maurice as the best available catch. Each year she had lowered the target of her ambition, after the Dominic fiasco set much too high, and she was beginning to fear that if she waited much longer she might find no one. She and Maurice had tastes in common. They both thought it of the first importance to have the best material conditions of life, and they liked to be in the swim and among the "right" people. He was pleased to marry the daughter of a rich peer, she to be supported in her own estimation of herself. He was six years older than she. Dominic was her own age.

Lord Dilton asked Maurice if his bath water was hot, which provoked Lady Dilton. For a few minutes Sylvia and Dominic were left to talk to each other.

"You've improved," she said bluntly, looking him in the eyes.

Their old familiarity was already waking between them.

In his own family Dominic was supposed to be dumb, stammering and full of violent irrational feeling, but away from their witty critical eyes he could often show a ready response, especially with women.

"So have you," he replied.

Sylvia was taken aback, but not displeased. His answer at once created the tension that she liked to feel with any good-looking man. But she thought that he was rather cool.

"You don't look as scrubby as I expected," she said.

"Then you did expect to see me."

"As you're in Father's regiment, it wouldn't be unnatural."

"But you wondered what I'd look like."

"I didn't lose any sleep over it."

"Why did you think I'd look scruffy?"

"Well, you've been in Australia for five years."

"Did you count them?"

"You're impossible," she said crossly, but she laughed.

Her parents stopped talking about the boiler and the conversation became general, pleasant, but a little dull. It was difficult to imagine Maurice taking part in any other kind of talk. When Lady Dilton and Sylvia left the room it became duller than ever. Lord Dilton seemed to find difficulty in calling his son-in-law by his Christian name, and slipped back into saying: "Having some port, Wesley-Maude?" Everything Maurice said and did was absolutely correct. He did not appear self-conscious but he inhibited any natural ease. He was, as Lady Dilton said, "a gentleman" and this was his religion. He would not dream of holding any view-point which was not correct, and so, though naturally honest, his character was at the mercy of the increasingly powerful forces that controlled opinion.

When they came into the drawing-room Maurice went correctly to pay attention to Lady Dilton. Lord Dilton talked for a few minutes to Sylvia and Dominic, then said: "I haven't had a chance to look at *The Times*," and left them together. Sylvia sat down on a gilt and yellow sofa on the far side of the fireplace, with a shaded lamp behind her.

Dominic was not used to much alcohol. At home he drank practically none, and in the mess very little, as he thought that he should not spend money that Helena might need. At dinner he had drunk a modest amount of claret and two glasses of port, and this was enough to stimulate his senses, and give him a glowing satisfaction with his surroundings.

"How do you like being home again?" asked Sylvia. She used the word "home" as when they had last met he had been their neighbour. Most Australians still called England "home", and Dominic would not have noticed the word if it had been used by anyone else, but coming from Sylvia it gave him a particular feeling which she had not intended.

He said that it was wonderful to be back, and that he hoped that the whole family would return to Waterpark after the war. She gave an involuntary exclamation of pleasure. Something passed between them. Dominic said, without knowing why: "I'm married too, you know."

"Yes. D'you like being married?"

"Of course. Don't you?"

"Naturally."

They laughed and suddenly stopped talking. Their old intimacy was reviving too quickly, in a way they had not foreseen, and now it had something added to it, an adult knowledge. They had never talked in this way before. They were both conscious that they might have been sitting here as man and wife. Dominic, like most people, hated losing anything that he had once had, but in him this feeling was very strongly developed. His childhood was spent in an atmosphere of loss, his family's losing money and leaving their house. Twice they had left Waterpark in an atmosphere of defeat. He had been a misfit at school and had failed in his army examination. Only on his farm in New South Wales did he escape this sense of loss. There they were gaining and building up. But at the moment it seemed very far away, a life so remote in every detail that it was more like something in his imagination than a reality. The present actuality always had most power for him, and his present actuality was extremely potent, even the purely material aspect of this magnificent room which could almost contain his whole farmhouse, but most of all, Sylvia, its living golden focus.

He was aware that if he had wanted it, she could have been his wife. He did not say to himself "if he had not been foolish", as he knew that his life with Helena was the best thing that could have happened for him. But he had lost his life with Sylvia and in a vague kind of way he wanted to make up for it, to retrieve some of the loss, in fact to have his cake and eat it. Flushed as he was with good wine he did not think this entirely impossible, though he had no conscious intentions. Part of his feelings was a simple pleasure at being friendly again with the Tunstalls, and the knowledge that at least one blot on his copybook was erased.

But mere friendship with Dominic would have bored Sylvia. Their fundamental views and interests were different. This had shown little during their engagement, and when it had, the gulf was bridged by physical attraction and their mutual interest in horses. She did not want men friends as cosy reminders of the schoolroom, and

2*

Dominic looked as if he could be far more than this. She too regarded him as something she had lost. If he had been as scrubby and colonial as her mother had said, she could have borne it, and one meeting to satisfy her curiosity would have been enough. But he was not scrubby or scruffy or whatever the word was. His dark eyes were lively with pleasure and admiration as he looked at her. The eyes of her husband, now talking to her mother about the connection between his family and the Wellesleys, never changed except to become red when he made love. She remembered how she used to feel when Dominic kissed her. One afternoon when they came in here after tennis – why, it was on this very sofa! Suddenly, in spite of herself, she gave an exclamation which sounded like annoyance, but was something deeper.

"What's the matter?" he asked.

"Nothing. I'd forgotten something."

Sylvia, as regards outward appearance, was as correct as her husband. She realized that this would not do – at any rate not here, and not yet. She began to talk with deliberate conventionality, repeating what various generals had said to her about the duration of the war. She asked about his parents, but did not mention Helena. Although normally there was no one of whom Dominic was more anxious to speak, he had no wish to do so with Sylvia.

Lord Dilton put down his paper and the conversation became general. When the parlour-maid brought in the whisky tray he said: "One for the road," and soon after that they left. When Dominic shook hands with Sylvia it was almost as if there was some hostility between them.

As they drove back to the depot, Lord Dilton, comfortable with drink, said: "I'm sorry you're not still at Waterpark." He meant that he was sorry that Dominic had not married Sylvia. He thought Maurice a dull dog.

[42]

About a month later the Wesley-Maudes came down again, for Maurice to say goodbye as he was on embarkation leave. Sylvia wrote telling her mother to ask Dominic to dine, and again he drove over from the depot with her father. Sylvia was on her guard this time, but Dominic was never on guard. He might behave conventionally, but when his passions smouldered, either with anger or love, it was evident. During dinner he showed that he was stimulated by her presence, and her mother heard some of the bantering exchange between them, and gave them a brief glance. Later, when the men came into the drawing-room, Dominic again sat by Sylvia who said: "You shouldn't reveal yourself so clearly."

"What have I revealed?" asked Dominic.

She was a little disconcerted. She was not yet prepared to go beyond allusion.

She did not give him any more exclusive attention that evening until he was leaving, when she managed to say without being overheard: "Come to see me when you are in London. I shall need cheering up." She gave him her address, adding: "Don't forget it."

"If I do, I can ask Lady Dilton," he replied.

"No. Don't do that," she said with a touch of irritation. "It's in the telephone book."

When next Lady Dilton saw her husband she said: "I think Dominic's too interested in Sylvia. I shouldn't bring him over while she's here. She'll probably be down quite a lot now Maurice has gone."

"That will be a bit difficult," said Lord Dilton. "I thought of putting him on the establishment."

"Why? He's young and healthy." She affirmed the principle underlying the 1914 war, which seemed to be the survival of the unfittest. Lord Dilton did not like being told by his wife how he should exercise his military responsibilities, but so far he had not voiced this intention. Dominic himself might not like it. He had not left his wife and child on the other side of the world to come and settle down in an English country town. He had often kicked over the traces but he was touchy about his honour. He was both straight and unpredictable, which amused Lord Dilton and was one of the reasons why he liked him. Still, if there was the risk of a romance between him and Sylvia, perhaps Edith was right, and it would be safer to say no more about it.

## CHAPTER FIVE

DOMINIC CONTINUED TO RECEIVE HELENA'S letters, and his replies were more than ever like the school-boy's, except that instead of "our second eleven beat Weldon's" he wrote: "Last night we were out on night-ops," or: "This afternoon we were on the range." He said no more about a return to Waterpark, and he told her that he had met Sylvia, who was married to a hussar, and living in London. He did not mention her a second time so Helena was at ease about the two things which had most worried her. She could write with more hope and spirit, trying, as she had begun, to keep before him their life together by giving the picture of its setting. He took his letters to his room to read, carefully absorbing every detail. Generally, he read them two or three times and he would sit lost awhile holding the letter and longing to be home. But he liked his army life. It interested him, and in an hour or two, or at any rate by the next morning the picture had become dim, and the life on the farm seemed to belong more to his past than his future.

Though by now the opposing trenches were firmly fixed, like two jaws mangling the youth of Europe, everyone except possibly some senior officers who hoped for higher promotion, and the war profiteers, hoped that the war would be over within a year. Helena allowed a year as the furthest possible date for Dominic's return. She put in plants that would bloom in a year's time. She wondered, if she set a rosemary hedge, whether there would be anything to show by then. But she not only did things to improve the garden and the house. She managed the farm as economically as possible so that they would have something to spend when he returned. Trying to keep him within the orbit of her life, she asked his advice, though he seldom replied to her questions. He was one of those correspondents who absorb without feeling the need to comment on what they are told. Sometimes she wrote, underlined:

*Please answer:*

*[a] It is hard to find men for the harvesting. Shall I get sheep and graze them? It would be good for the land.*

*[b] Do you want maize on the river flat, or should I graze that too?*

If he had replied, even disagreeing, she would have felt that he was *with* her. If he had said: "No, don't get any sheep. You'll have equal difficulty finding shearers. Buy bullocks. It would be wasteful to use the river flats for grazing." But he left the whole burden of management to her, when at least he could have shared the responsibility, if not the work. She tried not to blame him, as she knew that he could not express himself in letters, but she continued to feel that she was writing into a void. She did not know that her letters always created an hour or two of reverie and nostalgia in which he sent her all his love, though when the time came to reply he was back in the atmosphere of night-ops and rifle-ranges.

At last, towards the end of 1916, he was put on a draft for France, and given a week's embarkation leave. English subalterns generally went home for this, but Dominic had now no close relatives in England, beyond Cousin Emma, and Josie Wyckham, a first cousin who had married an English soldier a week or so before war was declared. He had recently been killed. Josie was living with his parents in Dorset, and Dominic did not like to suggest himself for a visit. He went up to London, to the little hotel in Mayfair. He called on Cousin Emma, which was not very exhilarating. She criticized his relatives in Australia for their indifference to the "right thing" and told him discreditable tales about his grandfather. She said that at first she had thought that Dominic would be "Australian", but now she nodded at his well-cut uniform with approval.

He then went to see Colonel Rodgers, who at last had been given a job at the War Office, but who had aged surprisingly in the last few months. He found himself quite unfitted for the office work of which it consisted. His memory was failing and a little later, after making innumerable blunders, he had to give up the job and return to Waterpark. The war was still his obsession and only topic of conversation. He said: "If only they'd give me a battalion at the front I'd be all right." If they had, he would doubtless have massacred it.

He asked Dominic to stay to dine at his club, and he moved the spoons and salt cellars about in battle formation. When they parted he said: "I don't suppose you've seen Sylvia."

"I saw her at Dilton with her husband," said Dominic.

"You know he's gone to the front? I shouldn't go to see her."

The white-haired angry old man turned and went off to the smoking room to find someone to fight the war with. Still with his wasp waist, his angular bony limbs, his eyes larger in his lean face, he was more like an insect than ever. As a boy Dominic had accepted his oddity, almost hero-worshipped him. Now for the first time in his life, looking at the colonel objectively, he thought that he was rather dreadful.

But with Colonel Rodgers and Cousin Emma he had exhausted his London friends, except Sylvia whom the colonel told him not to see. There were some more distant relatives, and that other colonel in the War Office, but he felt disinclined to look them up. For the first day he enjoyed the physical comfort of being on leave. It was nice to have his breakfast brought up by a pretty girl instead of being called by his soldier servant, and having to go across to the mess. He thought of asking the girl to go to the theatre with him; then he remembered Mrs Heseltine. He had lost her address but he remembered that her daughter was called Sherwood and lived at Wimbledon. He found her name in the telephone book and rang her up. The telephone was answered by Mrs Heseltine herself. She sounded surprised and not very pleased at hearing Dominic's voice. She was hurt that after their close friendship he had waited months to get in touch with her. Anyhow she could not possibly see him now, as her daughter had had a baby only the day before.

Before ringing off she relented a little and said: "Let me know when you're next in London." He did not tell her that he was going to France, and they did not meet again.

Dominic sat in his hotel bedroom with the prospect of six days before him, perhaps his last six in the civilized world, spent in mooning about in his own company. At first he had accepted Colonel Rodgers' injunction not to go to see Sylvia, thinking it would be wrong to intrude on her when she must be feeling as he felt in the first week after leaving Helena. Now he saw it as a flicker of the colonel's old jealousy. He took up the telephone and asked the girl at the desk to get him Sylvia's number.

Far from being in an abyss of depression, she sounded cheerful and very pleased to hear his voice.

"Where are you?" she asked.

When he told her she asked if he was free for luncheon, adding: "I am."

She suggested that they should lunch at the Ritz, as it was convenient for both of them. She would ring up for a table. They arranged that she should leave her house at one o'clock, and that he should walk down Green Park to meet her.

Dominic was a little disturbed that she had chosen the Ritz, again thinking of money that might go to Helena. As it turned out he need not have worried, as they could only eat as much as their food coupons allowed, and the Army authorities had fixed a modest limit to the amount officers might spend in restaurants.

He met Sylvia just inside the gates of the Park near Buckingham Palace. It was cold, but bright and sunny. She was wearing a dark coat with a sable collar, and a black velvet hat, so that her fair skin and her golden hair shone out as in some Renaissance portrait. As at Dilton he was startled when he saw her. He had not imagined that she would look like this in the daytime. In the evening, in yellow silk and pearls, amid the golden lights of the drawing-room at Dilton, it was natural that she should appear exquisite. He did not expect her to have the same effect in Green Park. Her clothes were simple but the people who passed glanced at her.

"This is fun," she said, shaking hands. "When did you come up?"

He told her that he had come on Sunday night, and that he was on embarkation leave.

"Why didn't you ring up before?"

"I had to go to see old Cousin Emma, and I dined with Colonel Rodgers."

"What, Uncle Marcus! How gay! Still, he always was my rival. And are you going to spend your leave with octogenarians?"

"No jolly fear," said Dominic. "Not if I can help it." He felt as if he had suddenly woken up, as if weights were lifted from his shoulders, as if grey doors enclosing him were flung open to the sun. They laughed and walked back up the park.

When they came into the Ritz restaurant they attracted notice, not only because of their good looks but because of the striking contrast between them: Dominic dark, arrogant and southern, Sylvia a pure gold product of the north. In a way this appearance was misleading, as Dominic's arrogance was intermittent, not like Sylvia's, an unchanging attitude; and her purity of intention was negligible, while his, confused and groping, remained constant. In spite of Sylvia's alleged poverty—and her appearance was one that only a rich woman can achieve—she seemed to be an *habituée* of the place, and they were deferentially led to a table in the window.

When they had ordered their food they looked at each

other and smiled, partly with pleasure, but also with surprise to find themselves there. It was so improbable, and it was new ground for them. At no time had they been together away from Dilton or Waterpark. They had a sense of new freedom, that in some way they were redeeming a failure. When they had drunk a little wine they took up again that allusive bickering kind of conversation they had begun when he dined at Dilton, and which was a new thing between them. Before, when they had been engaged, their love was adolescent, alternately blissful and angry. There was nothing amusing about it. They were like a man who has lost some money which later is not only returned to him, but returned with interest.

They were the last to leave the restaurant. In Piccadilly she asked him: "What are you doing now?"

"I have to buy some kit," he said.

"Shall I come and help you?"

"Yes, please do," he exclaimed eagerly. He had the idea that everything to do with Sylvia was related to sophisticated pleasure. That she was willing to do anything so humdrum as to choose army kit made her appear more simply human, and also more accessible. They went along to those stores which provided everything necessary for a Mayfair boudoir or a Flanders dugout; and even linked the two in special hampers of *foie gras* and French plums to send to young officers in the trenches.

She made him, as a matter of course, buy the most expensive things possible, and asked the shopman: "Are you sure this is the very best?" She really believed that by making him pay the highest price for every article, she was doing him a service, and later, when she had led him up to tea at Claridges, she said: "I don't believe you would have chosen nearly such good things if I had not come with you," which was true.

Dominic justified himself by thinking that all the things he had bought were for the trenches, and that Helena would not want him to economize on them. But this was only a passing thought. He, too, had Sylvia's taste for and expectation of the very best, though with him it reached beyond material things. The atmosphere that surrounded her was one most agreeable to himself. When he found himself in rich houses, both dignified and comfortable, where the best is normal, he felt that he was in his natural surroundings; though at home with Helena the idea of living in a palace like Dilton would have seemed absurd to him. Perhaps people of mixed blood have more varied nostalgias than those whose forebears were all of the same kind, living in the same place. From long generations of farming squires at Waterpark he found his deepest satisfactions on his own farm; from the Bynghams he inherited the impulse towards full-blooded bouts of extravagance; while from the Tebas he took his looks and his arrogance and his sombre passions, a taste for magnificence and the houses of the great. This is not romanticizing Dominic; he was already romantic, just as stark fact may often be. Sometimes stark facts made him act with the extreme of romanticism, as happened within a year.

He walked back with Sylvia to her house behind Buckingham Gate. Its drawing-room was no bigger than the green bath-room at Dilton, but it was furnished from the more magnificent rooms of that house, with a kingwood and ormolu commode and Italian mirrors. He had only come in to see the house, but he stayed until seven, when Sylvia had to change to dine out.

"I wish I could put it off," she said, "but it's impossible. Don't you know anyone under eighty with whom you can spend the evening?"

"I don't want to see anybody else," said Dominic. "It would spoil this afternoon."

They arranged to lunch again the next day, but at a different restaurant. Sylvia liked to be seen in public with Dominic, knowing that they were an arresting couple, but she was always discreet, and did not want to be seen with him twice in the same place. He said diffidently: "Am I taking up too much of your time?"

"Oh, no," she replied. "You mustn't waste your embarkation leave. I shall regard it as war work." He smiled but he looked a little hurt.

The next morning, with too much time to spend, he dawdled towards their appointment, looking in the shop windows and was ten minutes late. If any other man Sylvia knew had kept her waiting, after a few minutes she would have gone away, but the privilege of behaving uncertainly, which was one of the few things that Dominic had won for himself, acted even with her, and she only said, half amused: "You mustn't do this sort of thing you know."

"What sort of thing?"

"Keeping a woman waiting in a public place, or anywhere else as far as that goes."

"Am I late? I'm sorry," said Dominic, but he did not seem to realize the gravity of his offence.

When they sat down in the restaurant she was about to give him a short lecture, but restrained herself. In her first London season she had hoped to become engaged to a very good-looking eldest son, but he had not come up to scratch. An intimate friend told her that she was too bossy with him. She had said: "So often when one thinks one is being queenly, a reigning beauty, one is only being a governess; and a governess *per se* is never seductive." Sylvia was determined not to make this mistake with Dominic, particularly as she thought it was improbable that he would take it well.

In the afternoon she had to go to see an aunt at Hampton

Court, a promise she had made some time ago. She asked Dominic to come with her, but when they arrived she told him to go through and walk in the gardens while she visited her aunt. She would not stay long.

"It wouldn't do for you to come in," she said.

"Why, don't I look respectable?" asked Dominic.

"You are certainly presentable," said Sylvia, "but I don't know that you look exactly respectable. Anyhow, she's as blind as a bat."

"But isn't she Colonel Rodgers' sister? I ought to see her." Dominic was full of these friendly loyalties.

"She's also Mother's sister, and she'll tell her we came together. You must take a brisk walk. I'll meet you on the bridge in half-an-hour." She entered a little iron lift, which creaked perilously up through space to the top floor.

Dominic found his way out into the gardens, where the last leaves had fallen from the trees, and the borders were dug up and bare. He walked down towards the Long Water, and wondered why Sylvia, when she asked him to come down, had not told him that she did not want him to meet Mrs Pottinger, as her aunt was called—or rather, why Mrs Pottinger should not tell her mother that they had come down together. Though he often appeared erratic or worse to other people, in his own mind he was absolutely straight. When he concealed his actions or intentions, it was not from slyness, but simply because he forgot to mention them. Having been treated as a dunce when a boy, he always assumed that other people knew far more than he did, which showed even in his letters to Helena. But he hated the smallest deception between friends. He puckered his forehead as he thought that Sylvia had been a little sly. Then he found that for some odd reason this gave him a slight satisfaction. If her perfection had a slight flaw she was more accessible, though he did not yet know in what way he wanted her accessible. Anyhow it showed that she wanted his company, if only for the train journey. He went into the maze, and thinking of these things he lost himself, and was again ten minutes late in rejoining Sylvia, whom he found walking up and down beyond the bridge.

"You're incorrigible," she said. "I hurried away from Aunt Lizzie, saying I had an appointment, and one of her cronies has already passed me dawdling here."

"I got lost in the maze," he explained.

"But you oughtn't to go into the maze when you have to meet someone." She was being a governess, but with a half-amused exasperation.

"That's the sort of thing I do," said Dominic, partly apologetic, but more as if explaining an unalterable phenomenon.

"How on earth d'you get on in the army?"

"I only have to think about one thing at a time there. That's why it suits me."

"How many things do you have to think of now?"

"Only one."

"What is it?"

"You," he said.

He was smiling, and she laughed a little. He had said it for fun, for cheek, but it affected her more deeply.

In the evening they went to the theatre. During the war London enjoyed an uninterrupted season of four years, which spread from the rich through the whole community, enlivened by an excitement beyond peace-time imagination. Subalterns on a week's or a fortnight's leave, with six months' or a year's pay saved up in France, could live in a style they had never known as office workers. Everyone was kind to them and offered them hot baths, and those whose homes were far off spent their time in theatres and restaurants, and in the company of amiable but avaricious whores. These brief pleasures they earned in months of muddy sleepless nights, always in the shadow of death.

Dominic and Sylvia went to a rather sordid play about fallen women, which was the subject of so many jokes that they had thought it would be light fun. But Sylvia disliked the drab setting and the play itself stirred up the puritanism which was one of the dormant ingredients in Dominic's make-up. If the ultimate result of his actions was revealed to him he could not help taking it into account. Until they saw this play he had no clear intention of his relationship with Sylvia becoming more intimate. He thought that it was just friendship and old affection. The play made him think of the possibility, at the same time giving him a feeling of its sordidness, which was increased when he remembered her slight deception of her aunt that afternoon. They both felt a little flat as he took her back to Catherine Street. He said goodnight, and she did not ask him in. He said that the next day he was lunching with Cousin Emma. She made no comment but as she was about to close the door, she said: "Then come to tea at five."

In the morning he went to the bank for his letters. There was one from his father saying that as he might have extra expenses going to the Front he was sending him a hundred pounds. Steven's real reason for sending this money was that he had had a letter from Lord Dilton saying how pleased he was to have Dominic as a subaltern, and what an excellent officer he made. Steven thought of Dominic's difficulties as a boy, and although he had treated him with the extremes of patient good intention, he now accused himself of not having understood him properly. He was also ashamed that his sons had to go to war, while his own life had been spent in absolute safety, and he had never

[55]

fired a gun at anything but a partridge or a rabbit. The only gesture he could make was to send them money.

Helena's letter mostly described the baby learning to walk on the verandah, which was shaded by a Gloire de Dijon rose, tangled with a vine and a peach tree. At the moment the three were a riot of flowers and fruit and when the afternoon sun filtered through them the colour was brilliant. When two potent but inconsistent ideas entered Dominic's mind together, they caused a kind of jam or stoppage that was almost a physical pain. Helena's letter wakened vivid images inconsistent with the life he had led for the past few days. While he read it he was entirely with her, longing to be back with her in that simple happy life on his own land. When he had finished he read it again, and then sitting on the mahogany chair in the bank, he fell into one of those dreams of home, and the clerk watching him again wondered if his news was good or bad.

At luncheon with Cousin Emma he talked a great deal about Helena and his home, which did not interest her as his establishment did not sound elegant, and she asked why he had fruit trees growing so close to the house. She was more interested in the names of the officers in his regiment, and she asked him if he had been again to Dilton, and he told her only to dine.

"Have you seen that girl you were engaged to?" she asked, giving him a sharp, old woman's glance.

"Yes," said Dominic. "She's married. She lives in London."

"Do you see her?"

"Yes," said Dominic.

Cousin Emma changed the subject. When he left she came with him to the door. Dominic, living for two or three months as a student in her house, had driven her nearly crazy; but she now felt an affection for him, especially as he was handsome, "smart", and going to the front.

"Let me know your address in France," she said, "and I'll send you a plum cake from Harrods."

Dominic walked from Brompton Square to Catherine Street, as he had time to fill in. His mind was full of the associations of his family and his home. His father's kindness in sending him the money, when he knew that he had little to spare; the unexpected glimpse of Cousin Emma's affection when he had always thought of her as worldly and censorious; above all Helena's letter, created a picture in his mind in which Sylvia had no part. When he did think of her she was even destructive of the picture. She blotted it out. The alliance with the Tunstalls would have been disproportionate to the Langtons' way of life. It would have disrupted it, like a patch of new cloth on an old garment. When the engagement was broken the family recovered its integrity. He remembered the scene at Waterpark when Sylvia had given him back his ring— the faint amusement and relief, coupled with regret that Dominic had lost such a prize. They returned to their home on the other side of the world, and within a month he was married to Helena. Now Australia appeared to him as his natural setting. Over the past fifty years the successive returns to Waterpark had always ended in misfortune, and Steven was right to refuse to live there again. He forgot his own enthusiasm for this project a few months earlier, a reaction from the six weeks' misery on the ship.

Trying to take a short cut between Sloane Street and Grosvenor Place, he lost himself, and he compared it with being lost in the bush. His nostrils ached for the smell of gum trees. He saw the war as something he must endure to save the easy friendly life of his parents at Westhill, and of his wife and child on their farm. To Sylvia it seemed to be the occasion for a life of pleasure in London, with "war work" as the entertainment of officers in a succession of lunches at the Ritz. He felt towards her as a child feels when having made friends with a stranger, it meets some of its own group, and treats its new friend with indifference or even hostility.

When he arrived at Catherine Street she seemed to have the same feeling, though really she was bothered by the change in Dominic. She saw that he had gone from her, that something had happened to him, and she put it down to the play last night, knowing nothing of the influence of his letters from home. She knew from their past association that he was capable of sudden severe moral judgements, but she was never quite sure what provoked them. They were unrelated to the code in which she had been trained, and which she had boiled down to "never be found out". From their near-intimacy, which she was prepared to complete, and from the way in which their conversation had immediately become allusive, she thought that he had passed through these moral phases, that he had "grown up", and that his attitude was much the same as her own. She did not realize that in any relationship there is always a "third party risk", that a person unknown may say something to a man or woman which changes the attitude to a friend or lover. With Dominic the third party risk was one which she might have foreseen, a letter from Helena.

During tea he was silent and she was stilted, openly "governessy". She almost wanted to get rid of him, she had cancelled all her engagements for the remaining days of his leave, but she was not prepared to let him treat her casually. No man might do that. To awaken some kind of response she said: "I may have to go down to Dilton tomorrow. Mother's not very well."

Dominic looked a little surprised, but he only said: "Oh, I'm sorry," and she did not know whether he was sorry because she was going or because her mother was unwell. She said with a touch of contempt, to point out that if she went away he would have only elderly relatives to entertain him: "Did you enjoy your lunch with Lady Langton?"

"Yes. She was awfully kind," he answered, not seeing her intention, but thinking she was trying to bring herself, also with kind motives, into the picture which filled his mind. He smiled for the first time since he had come in, and said: "She's going to send me a plum cake from Harrods."

The atmosphere eased. The mutual repudiation evaporated and they began to talk again with their easy, amused bickering, and to Dominic their relationship immediately became innocent. As long as he behaved instinctively he felt that he was innocent. When he was made to think of what he was doing, especially by something like the squalid play, he fell back on the Calvinism imposed on him in his childhood. With his ever ready generosity he was anxious to make up for his unfairness to Sylvia, while she, relieved to find that he had only been in "one of his moods", wanted to pretend that nothing had happened. Outwardly this was so, as their quarrel had consisted entirely of telepathic waves of reconciliation, and a new degree of intimacy was achieved. They felt safer with each other.

For the next three days they spent their whole time together. Dominic felt more strongly that something of his own was being restored to him. In the evening, if they stayed in, she showed him before dinner into the bathroom which opened off her own room, and she lent him Maurice's spare hair brushes. He waited alone in the drawing-room while she changed, and examining at his leisure its toy palatial perfection, he thought that if he had wanted to he could be living here as her husband. For the house was not Maurice's, but, like everything in it, given to her by her father. Vaguely he felt that he had a prior right to it.

They no longer bothered to go to places of amusement. On the Saturday afternoon they walked through the parks and had tea at a shop at Notting Hill Gate. Dominic wanted to return on the top of a 52 bus, but Sylvia never travelled in buses. She gave the reason that it would be too cold, but her real one, apart from her prejudice against them, was that it would be too conspicuous.

Dominic was to leave for France by a train leaving Victoria at seven o'clock on Monday morning. When they returned from Notting Hill Gate he told Sylvia that he would like to go to church the next morning, Sunday. Conventional people, whatever their belief, still went regularly to church. Dominic had the idea that the eve of his departure to fight for his country was an occasion that required a form of knightly dedication. He asked Sylvia to go with him.

"To church?" she asked, surprised. "Very well, but where can we go?"

"There are plenty of churches. Where do you go?"

Sylvia went to St Mark's, North Audley Street, which had the richest and smartest congregation in London. In the porch on the Sunday before Ascot one could hear them discussing the form of racehorses. She did not want to go there with Dominic, and be seen by her friends. At first she had been pleased at the quick glances or frank stares of admiration which they attracted, but since the afternoon at Hampton Court she had kept away from places where they might be known.

"There's a church by Brompton Square," she said. "People are married there sometimes."

"Yes. It's behind Cousin Emma's house," said Dominic.

"Does she go there?" asked Sylvia quickly.

"No. She's a Roman Catholic. She goes to the Oratory."

They arranged that he would call for her at half past ten. While they were in the atmosphere of arrangement, Sylvia put forward a suggestion which she had been waiting for an opportunity to make easily.

"Wouldn't it be better," she said, "if you stayed here tomorrow night? It's so much closer to Victoria. You could put your heavy luggage in the cloakroom in the afternoon, and walk to the station in the morning, without having to bother about the risk of not finding a taxi at that hour."

"Thank you. That will be much nicer," said Dominic. "It will be rather fun."

Sylvia was puzzled, wondering what he meant by fun.

In the morning they went to Holy Trinity, Brompton, where they sat through the unexacting performance of Matins, and a sermon which was concerned more with the war than the Christian religion. After this there was a celebration of Holy Communion, in the middle of which half the congregation rose to leave, Sylvia with them. She had an intense dislike of going to Communion, and only did so to please her mother, if she happened to be at Dilton at Christmas or Easter. Dominic, still intent on his knightly dedication, murmured that he was "going to stay". He was in some way both consecrating and saying farewell to all the associations of his life hitherto, offering them in defence of the freedom without which life is worthless. Sylvia could not bring herself to kneel beside him through this rite. It would be an impossibly Catholic form of intimacy, almost indecent. A public prostitute might have done so, conscious of her sins, but untroubled by any inconsistency. Dominic, although his religious teaching had been more Calvinistic than Sylvia's, had more the nature of the Catholic prostitute. He did not divide life into separate compartments, where the inconsistencies were accepted but kept in isolation. He wanted it all related and unified.

[61]

"I'll wait outside," said Sylvia. She went out and strolled up and down the path at the side of the Oratory. She thought Dominic impossible. Why did he choose to go to Holy Communion when he had arranged to spend the night with her? What did he mean by "rather fun"? In the last few days there had been accidental, or not quite accidental physical contacts between them. Desire was in their finger-tips. Or was she mistaken? No, she could not be. Tonight things must take their inevitable course. Then why must he commit this vulgarity?

She was in a state of irritation when with a dozen or so older people he came out of the church.

"Now let's go to the Ritz," he said cheerfully. She gave up trying to understand him. She had been afraid that he would be in a solemn or priggish mood, but his act of dedication seemed to have left little effect.

In the Brompton Road they ran into Cousin Emma coming from a late Mass. Sylvia, who knew her by sight, tried to avoid her, but Dominic deliberately drew her attention and introduced them. He even asked her to join them at luncheon, but she said that she had "one of Coco's boys", a General Somebody, coming to lunch with her. She looked at Sylvia with complete approval, and telling Dominic that she would not forget the plum cake, she once more said goodbye.

Sylvia, who normally regarded herself as the capable mistress of any situation, felt herself becoming dumb. Would he next suggest that she should ring up Uncle Marcus and ask him to dine with them? They walked in silence up the Brompton Road, Dominic pleased that he had been able to show her off to Cousin Emma, who had obviously been impressed. At last Sylvia burst out: "Can't you say something?"

"What d'you want me to say?" he asked, surprised and a little amused. It pleased him to see her disturbed, in the same way that it had pleased him when she had deceived Mrs Pottinger.

"Anything, rather than walk along like a deaf mute."

" 'To walk in silence develops the inner life'," said Dominic, which was a quotation used as a joke in his family.

"What is the inner life?" she asked.

"Do you mean mine, or inner life generally?"

"Yours at the moment."

"I don't know. We have to discover our inner lives."

"When shall we do that?" She was amused at a conversation so akin to her usual style.

He looked at her and said impudently: "Tonight perhaps."

She almost stopped, and she could not speak for a minute. But she still thought it possible that he only meant in a conversation over the dinner table.

In the afternoon they went to the little Mayfair Hotel to collect his luggage, and took it to Victoria Station. From there, Dominic carrying a small case, they walked the few hundred yards to Catherine Street, and did not go out again. At seven o'clock there was a break in their propinquity while Sylvia went to change. During dinner she talked about food in war-time, which for her was no problem. She had chickens, game, butter and cream sent up from Dilton. There was a pheasant for dinner.

They were not like lovers, neither excited nor particularly tender. They were more like two people filling in time before a pleasant appointment. After dinner she told him some of the criminal slanders on the Prime Minister, which were circulating in Tory society and which he had already heard from Colonel Rodgers. She believed them herself, and Dominic accepted them as curious information about a sphere outside his knowledge or interest.

The parlourmaid who waited on them saw no reason to question Sylvia's statement: "My cousin Mr Langton will stay tonight, as he must catch the boat train early in the morning." There was a tenuous connection between the Langtons and the Tunstalls which excused her mentioning a relationship. Her brothers and one or two other relatives had stayed there to catch the early train.

At ten o'clock they went to bed. There was nowhere for Dominic to sleep, except in Maurice's dressing-room. The drawing-room took up the floor below and the servants occupied the attic above. Sylvia, in a loose garment edged with swansdown, put her head round the door and said: "You can have the bathroom now."

When he came back from the bath, the door into her room was open, and from it shone a dim rosy light. He went in to her. She was lying on the bed, looking as he had imagined her when he lay in the bath on that first night at Dilton.

The uncertainties which had irritated Sylvia during the day, giving her, as in the Brompton Road, a sense of frustration, during the evening had evaporated. Dominic's "inner life", the dynamo which she imagined as purring in him, had been accumulating power. They were both aware of its vibrations, and if she had not left her door ajar, confident in his power, he would have opened it.

As he lay beside her she put out her hand to switch off the light, but he caught it and the rosy glow remained. He wanted to see this rare and delicate beauty, his former right restored to him. He felt that at last he possessed all that he rightly owned, the other part of his double world, making it complete.

Sylvia, her mind stimulated, lay awake beside him. She thought about him, wondering about the uncertainties she had felt, now obliterated by this certainty. She was sure that she would never feel them again. She thought that at last she understood him. He performed most of his actions without reasoning about them. He did not, having recognized the inconsistencies of life, keep them in separate watertight compartments, but left the doors open between them. This was what made him so unpredictable, but also so attractive. It gave him the integrity of something untamed, the kind of savage innocence of a creature still observing the laws of the natural world.

She put out the light, and as he breathed softly and deeply beside her, she felt almost as if she were in some indefinable natural lair. He was like a dark sun, bathing her with warmth, his rays flooding her whole body with a new vitality drawn from some primitive source. She lay close against him, receiving his rays, and she felt that she had received all his mystery.

She had borrowed the servants' alarm clock, giving as the reason that they might sleep through its ringing, as they had sometimes done, and that it was of vital importance for Dominic to catch the train. When this tinny contraption, standing on a dressing-table said to have come from the Grand Trianon, stabbed the air with its warning, she shook Dominic out of his heavy sleep. Drowsily he made as if to embrace her, but she gave him one long kiss, and then became matter-of-fact. She sent him to the bed in the dressing-room, and went up to call her maid, who in half an hour, brought up separate trays of tea and toast to their rooms.

Still brisk and cheerful, she went with Dominic to Victoria. He was a little dazed. He had not stepped so neatly from one watertight compartment to another. His doors were all open.

They collected his luggage from the cloakroom, and followed by a porter wheeling it, came to the boat-train.

On the platform was a subaltern from the depot, who was on the same draft as Dominic. He was expecting him and had kept two seats in a Pullman. When he saw Sylvia with Dominic whom he knew was married, he thought that she must be his wife. He greeted them cheerfully, but with a delicate nuance for their approaching separation, and having pointed out the seats in the Pullman, he entered the train and rearranged his luggage, to leave them alone together.

"Is that young man from the depot?" asked Sylvia sharply.

"Yes," said Dominic, and she told him not to say who she was.

"What is his name?" she asked.

Dominic told her that he was called Hollis.

## CHAPTER SIX

HOLLIS WAS JUST NINETEEN YEARS OF AGE AND THE son of Lord Dilton's lawyer in Salisbury. If there had been no war he would have been learning his father's profession. He had left school six months earlier and was excited at being on his way to a war. He had stayed the night alone at the Grosvenor Hotel, which was an enlargement of his experience, as was also the unaccustomed luxury of having his breakfast in a Pullman. His life hitherto had been spent between the monastic seclusion of his public school, and the domestic simplicity of his home. He had the naïve sensual innocence, the retarded emotional development of many boys of his kind of upbringing, which at his age gave them a certain charm. Going to the war, he imagined that he was now a man, though those who saw him in his smart new uniform, his Sam Browne belt not yet mellow and supple with use, found piquancy in the contrast of his baby face with his accoutrements, like that of a *putto* in an Italian painting, wearing the helmet and playing with the lance of Mars. This poetic conjunction of the ideas of youth and death was found in the popular verse of the time. One sang:

> *Take my youth that died today,*
> *Lay him on a roseleaf bed.*

Another, more hearty, declared:

> *With the milk on their mouths*
> *And the time on their wrists . . .*
> *They spread the honour thick on the roll,*
> *His Majesty's second-lieutenants!*

Another advised the boy to rejoice in his fate:

> *Earth that blossomed and was glad*
> *'Neath the cross that Christ had,*
> *Shall rejoice and blossom too*
> *When the bullet reaches you.*
> *Therefore men marching*
> *On the road to death, sing.*
> *Pour out gladness on earth's head,*
> *So be merry, so be dead!*

Julian Grenfell wrote:

> *The blackbird sings to him; Sing brother, sing,*
> *If this shall be the last song you sing . . .*
> *Who dies fighting hath increase.*

Mr Max Beerbohm later wrote a story about a starry-eyed young war poet, who to the disgust of his public did not get killed, and so achieve in his person the sacrificial beauty of his poems.

Though Hollis knew that he was entering the Moloch jaws of the opposing trenches, where so many of his kind were spreading honour on the roll, he went there surrounded by so much indulgence, praise and unaccustomed social privilege that in spite of the popular poems, they diminished the secret dread that he might be killed. He wanted to talk about it all, and said things like: "I bet my young brother will be envious when he gets a letter from me stamped 'On Active Service'."

He said: "I've never had a meal on a train before. It's a good way to go to a war. It makes you feel cosmopolitan."

He also said: "French girls are pretty good, aren't they?"

At last Dominic said: "Shut up!" Hollis blushed. He realized that he should not have said this to Dominic who was married, and who, he imagined, had just parted from his wife.

While Hollis was eating everything available to increase his cosmopolitan feeling, Dominic drank only a cup of coffee. When Hollis stopped talking he laid his head against the back of his chair, and appeared to doze all the way to Folkestone. He was sunk in semi-conscious reverie, satisfied and relaxed. Not only his physical senses but his pride was satisfied. In the warm carriage the sense of Sylvia's nearness was with him, soothed by the rhythm of the train.

Hollis thought that he was an odd chap. At the depot he had not had much to do with him, as they were in different companies, and in the mess Dominic talked to older men. Now he looked at his sleeping face, at the rather long jaw, the wide mouth, of which the curves had a voluptuous emphasis in relaxation. The heavy eyelids sloped downwards, giving him a look of sorrow in sleep. Hollis thought he looked jolly interesting, and wished that he had the same sombre lines of experience. He thought that his own rosy cheeks and shining hair were sickeningly puerile.

When they left the train for the boat at Folkestone, the fresh air and the bustle brought Dominic back to brisk life and action. At last he identified his interests with Hollis's. They struggled together on to the crowded boat, and found a corner for their luggage. They helped each other on with their life-belts, and sat on their rolled-up valises watching the silvery "blimp" which flew past them, on the lookout for submarines.

At Calais, after much fuss, delay and direction, they found themselves on a curious little island in the midst of a vast expanse of railway lines. Here there were a few subalterns from other regiments, and a little shed with "*Buvette*" written on it, where stale rolls, coffee and oranges were sold. Late in the evening, they entered a train for Etaples, arriving at one o'clock the next morning. They groped through the darkness for half a mile or so to an army hut, where nothing happened for twenty minutes. Then an officer appeared and told them they had to go somewhere else, down in the town. Hollis was in that state of fatigue when any further frustration appears ludicrous, and he began to laugh. One of the other subalterns turned on him with angry insolence. He saw truly that if once the soldier began to laugh at the futility of much of his activity, the war could not continue. Hollis, without any undisciplined intention, had offended in this.

Dominic too was exhausted, not only from the past day, but from his passion on the previous night; and was now in a state of irritable sensitivity. With his absolute loyalty to his own kind, he would at any time have been annoyed at a man from another regiment speaking in that way to his fellow-subaltern. But in his present emotional condition, heightened by his physical exhaustion, he flared out: "D'you want your damned head knocked off?"

The captain glanced up from the table where he was writing on some form, but when he saw the look in Dominic's eyes he said nothing. The subaltern who had rebuked Hollis looked both indignant and scared. He muttered and turned away.

The party left the hut and walked down through the darkness to their billets, Dominic and Hollis a few yards behind.

"Why did you let fly like that?" asked Hollis.

"I don't know. It happens to me sometimes," said Dominic.

"I hope you don't do it to me. I thought you were going to knife him."

"I don't do it to my friends."

At the end of this shared and curious day, warmed perhaps by the blaze of Dominic's anger, a friendship had sprung up between them, of which there had been no sign when they set out. Dominic felt that he had taken Hollis under his protection. They followed the others through the darkness, comfortable in the knowledge of their friendship.

Dominic thought that he had been moved by loyalty to Hollis, and by his dislike of the type of the other man, but it was something far deeper that had aroused his anger, something that was latent in him like a diamond in a mass of coal, which did not begin to take shape until the following autumn.

At Etaples they were put through three days of intensive preparation for the trenches, throwing live bombs and stumbling, choking in inadequate masks, through gas-filled tunnels cut in the sand-dunes of the "bull-ring". There was a rumour amongst the soldiers, probably with little foundation, that one man a day was killed there.

After this Dominic and Hollis were put in charge of a draft of men to go up to the front. The decrepit train with broken windows crawled along through the snow. It took twelve hours to go thirty miles, so that when they arrived they felt that they had travelled half-way across Europe. Some of the men lighted braziers in their carriages. They kept hopping out of the crawling train to collect fuel. For the officers it was like travelling in charge of a crate of escaping cats.

They reached Béthune after dark. While they were marshalling their men on the railway station they heard the sound of distant gun-fire. It made Hollis apprehensive, but it excited Dominic, making him feel noble and important, and about to find the fulfilment of his existence in its reason, in fighting evil. His first approach to everything was romantic, and then slowly he had to discover its reality. His approach to Sylvia was entirely romantic and he had not yet found her reality. His approach to Helena was both real and romantic at the same time. What he saw in her and gave romantic worship to, was the reality he had known since childhood. She was not a symbol of anything, not a compensation for frustrations in his adolescence, whereas Sylvia was almost entirely a symbol and a compensation.

They spent a week billeted in peasants' cottages, and drilling in frozen fields on the outskirts of Béthune. Then at last they were sent to join the first battalion in the trenches, travelling to Noeux-les-Mines on the top of a London bus. Here they reported to the transport officer. Outside his quarters there was a shell hole in a neatly planted onion bed. The peasants were still living in their cottages, some damaged by shell-fire, only a mile or so from the front line, so firmly fixed were the opposing trenches. If after an attack one side gained a hundred yards, the victory was a misfortune, as the newly captured trenches had their dugouts and parapets on the wrong side, and were more receptive to enemy shells.

When it was dark Dominic and Hollis set out with a sergeant as guide to the front line, stumbling along through the seemingly uncharted wastes of a ruined country, until they descended into the communication trenches. Although they had heard the gunfire at Béthune, this part of the line, having been drenched with its share of blood in the Battle of Loos, was now quiescent. The darkness was occasionally broken by the eerie flare of Verey lights, to illuminate any hostile prowlers. The scene was already familiar from photographs and comic cartoons in the illustrated papers.

At last they were shown down some steps and through a sacking curtain into a dugout, where Burns, the company commander, and a second lieutenant called Frost were waiting for their arrival to begin dinner. This meal, which was served by two officers' servants from another dugout, consisted of grilled soles, pork chops, apple tart and cream. They drank Vichy water and white wine, which did not need cooling as some of the bottles had already frozen and had cracked.

Burns was friendly and very pleased to see them, as in these quiet trenches only one officer had to be on a watch at night. He shared this duty with Frost, and the arrival of two new subalterns would double the hours of their sleep. Frost, although he welcomed this, was a little indignant at territorial officers being posted to the first battalion, and he addressed them rather superciliously.

Dominic and Hollis had the easiest possible introduction to the war, except for the extreme cold. For two or three months nothing spectacular happened, beyond the routine of a week in the front line, a week in the reserve trenches, and a week in one of the villages close behind the line. Occasionally a man might be killed or wounded by a stray shell or a trench mortar. Two or three times there were heavy barrages in which men were killed, but no raid followed. In more realistic periods of history the opposing commanders would have agreed to move into winter quarters, but the powers-that-be were afraid that their armies might lose "the spirit of the offensive".

Towards the end of this calm, cold period Burns, strolling along the reserve trench on a sunny April morning, was blown to pieces by a stray shell, almost the only one to explode in their sector on that day. When they came out of the trenches at the end of the week, they were given a new company commander called Harrison. He had been slightly wounded a few months earlier and had only just returned from England. Like Frost, he was annoyed at having territorial officers under him and almost his first remark to Dominic and to Hollis was an order to take off the "T's" under the regimental badges on their lapels. Out of the line he was more of a martinet than Burns had been, but in the trenches he became nervous. His wound, though slight, had been very painful, and he did not want it to happen again. He did not take any of the night watch, and when there was much shell-fire he stayed in his dugout. It so happened that his appointment as company commander coincided with the hotting-up of the war.

If Dominic had met Harrison under any other circumstances he would probably have avoided him, but here it was impossible. They were forced together for weeks on end in the intimacy of dugouts and cottage billets. With the official enemy a hundred yards away beyond the barbed wire and the pitted earth, a far greater enmity arose between them, greatest on Dominic's side. Harrison was again the type that he detested. They differed in every way, but in one most particularly. Dominic had to grope through his romanticism to the reality behind it; whereas Harrison had to approach reality from the other side, passing through the protection given by complete lack of imagination, until the hearty words which had given him courage had lost their meaning. This had already happened and he sweated in his dugout. He applied no imagination to Dominic, who was both an Australian and a territorial, and therefore Harrison thought, unquestionably his inferior. He saw no reason to conceal anything so self-evident.

The conversation of the young officers was more than half the time about women. Sometimes, though Dominic had no intention of joining their excursions in search of sensual pleasure behind the lines, his desires were aroused, and he thought that Sylvia would be waiting for him when he went on leave. Harrison boasted of the number of women he had had, and kept a walking stick on which he made a notch for each of them, now seventy-four in number. While he boasted Dominic sat aloof, and Harrison said: "I don't suppose you like your damned aristocratic company commander."

Soon after this the sappers tunnelling under the enemy trenches came to within a few feet of a German dugout. They could hear talking and laughing. The company had to provide an officer and a few men to put explosives under the dugout and annihilate its occupants. Harrison asked for volunteers from among his three subalterns and Dominic offered. He had left his home to fight for his country and for the values of civilization, but so far he had done little more than sit in a dugout and listen to talk about sex. Here at last was something that would justify the "O.A.S." on his envelopes.

With their dangerous equipment he and his men crept stealthily along the tunnel until they came to where they could hear the Germans talking. Dominic, with that curiosity about humanity which governed so many of his actions, did not immediately do the job and hurry away. He signed to his men to wait while he listened to the voices from the dugout. He heard the clink of glasses and a man's quiet contented laugh. He imagined the scene much as it was in their own dugout, when they came in for a drink during a night watch. His men were impatient to get away, but they thought that he was listening for useful information, not merely to realize his common humanity with the men he was about to destroy.

At last they set their torpedoes and fled. Soon they were rewarded by the sound of the explosion. Dominic went to Harrison and reported that the operation was successful. Harrison for once was very pleased with him and said that for this and his good routine work in the trenches he would suggest him for one of the next Military Crosses awarded to the battalion. Dominic, as so often in his life, as soon as he had won approval, immediately but unconsciously did something to lessen it. He was sweating and looked disturbed.

"Anyhow," he said, "they would die instantly."

"What has that got to do with it?" asked Harrison sharply. Dominic was either gloating over his victims, which was in bad taste, or he had introduced a consideration which was impossible for a soldier.

When he came out of the line he had a letter from Helena, also replies from Sylvia and Cousin Emma. The latter had been to a charity matinée, explaining that "one must keep the flag flying". Sylvia's letter was also about social activities, but like the other short notes she had written him, it ended "with love". Receiving letters from Helena and Sylvia produced one of those jams in his brain, due to the conflict of irreconcilable ideas. Strangely his infidelity to Helena had not troubled him before. Sylvia had been more the fulfilment of a youthful ambition, the payment of a debt owing to him, than an infidelity. She was also perhaps the satisfaction of a physical necessity for a hot-blooded young man separated from his wife. She may have regarded him in the same way, as her letters suggested not so much the longings of a separated lover, but that she was retaining a lien on him.

He left Sylvia's and Cousin Emma's letters on his bed, and taking Helena's he walked across the fields to a neighbouring village, and went to the church to read it. It was a kind of reassurance to himself that his only true fidelity was to Helena. Her letter must be read separately, in this quiet and sacred place, where the trees in the churchyard were bursting into green. He picked a bud from a chestnut tree, and laid it on the step beside him, while he opened her letter. It was one of the least cheerful he had had from her. Soon the sheep would have to be dipped and she had not enough labour for it. She had dismissed Harry, as he was now old enough to go to the war, but would not enlist. Dominic felt ashamed that she had these cares, and yet for the first time since he left, in fact almost for the first time in his life, he felt annoyed with her. Why had she dismissed Harry without asking him? He had explicitly stated that Harry was to remain and help her till he returned. Although he depended so much on Helena and nearly always followed her advice, when he had made a decision in his own department he expected it to be followed. He would not have dismissed one of her maids.

He sat despondently on the church steps, dangling the letter. Idly he picked up the chestnut bud and examined it, becoming absorbed in its delicate beauty, the mysterious unfolding of the young leaves. As he looked at it, he was reminded of the curling fingers of his son when he held him soon after he was born. He forgot where he was sitting. Something like the feeling he had when he watched the Spanish divers, that there was no division between man and the natural world, returned to him. He had a curious feeling of contentment which was disturbed by the thin whine of a shell sailing high above him toward the German lines. With the blackbirds, death moaned and sang in the spring air. The bursting green of the trees, of the bud he held in his hand, was only a symbol of the resurgence of war. He threw the bud into the grass, and set out to walk back to the company billets.

At the door of the mess he met Hollis, who wanted him to come and dine with him in Béthune. They obtained permission and set out to walk the few miles into the old town, which was not reduced to a heap of rubble until a year later.

They went first to the Officers' Club for a drink, and then to dine at the Hôtel de France. During dinner they shared a bottle of burgundy. Their conversation became cheerful and intimate. Hollis said he wanted to visit a whore. He said: "It would be awful to get killed before you'd done it." Dominic discouraged him, not so much on moral grounds but because he had a poetic feeling that Hollis's innocence should not be wasted on a prostitute. It was due to the lingering of the mood which possessed him as he held the leaf, the sense that our bodies were of the same nature as all creative life, that they should function in innocence, and not as the result of a commercial transaction. They dawdled over their dinner, and then set out to walk back to the company. They came to an orchard by the side of the road. The trees, covered with blossoms, were like beautiful girls in the moonlight.

"Let us sit down here for a bit," said Hollis, and they sat on the top rail of the fence. The moon was bright enough for Dominic to see the left side of Hollis's face, which looked very sad.

They heard the thin whine of a shell far above them, and after a few minutes another. They were falling on Béthune.

"We just got out in time," said Dominic.

"I would have looked damn silly dead in a whore-house," said Hollis. "I'm jolly glad you dissuaded me." They were silent again and at intervals two more shells passed overhead.

Hollis said:

> *There's not the smallest orb that thou beholdest*
> *But in its motion like an angel sings,*
> *Still quiring to the young-eyed cherubim.*

"Where did you learn that?" asked Dominic curiously.

"At school, I suppose. I just remembered it."

"Oh God!" said Dominic.

"What's up?"

"Our hellish lives."

He sat on the top rail with his head in his hands and his elbows on his knees. Then he suddenly climbed over into the orchard, and walked away among the clouds of blossom.

"Where are you going?" asked Hollis. He vaulted the fence and followed him.

Dominic stopped in a secluded hollow in the centre of the orchard. He unfastened his Sam Browne belt, and then took off his tunic, flinging them on the ground. He undid his boots and kicked them off, and finally stripped off his remaining clothes.

"What are you doing? You're mad," said Hollis uncertainly.

"I want to breathe. I can't breathe in those things," said Dominic. He stretched his arms and buried his face in the blossom. Hollis watched him, and then, as if hypnotised, discarded his own clothes. He danced with his bare feet in the wet grass, and said: "I'll race you," and they ran between the lines of trees. Hollis flung himself on the grass where he rolled over and over in the dew, and then sat up laughing, and dried himself on his khaki handkerchief.

"Listen," said Dominic. The two young men stood naked, restored to innocence in the stillness of the natural world. There was no sound, and yet it seemed that the stillness was full of sound beyond their perception, the sound of life growing in the trees, and thrusting up the young blades of grass. Hollis was going to say: "We are like the Greeks," but he could not speak. There was something in the night far beyond this allusion, and he felt not only would it be wrong to speak, but that if he did his voice would break beyond his control. "I wish we could stay here for ever," he said at last. They wandered about among the trees for a while, but soon it became chilly, and they dressed and climbed back on to the road.

On the night before the battalion was due to return to the front line, Dominic and Hollis again had permission to go to dine in Béthune; and again after dinner Hollis said that he wanted to visit a whore. Dominic automatically advanced his objections, but then he thought of Harry dismissed, of the Germans he had blown up, of all the young men with the milk on their mouths poured into the Moloch jaws. Let them have any reward they could grab.

He did not go with prostitutes himself, partly from fastidi-ousness, and partly from fidelity, either to Helena or Sylvia or both; but Hollis's situation was different.

"I don't see why the devil you shouldn't," he said. "But where can you find one?"

"There's a place with a red light in a cul-de-sac not far away."

"Good God, you can't go there!" said Dominic. "It's only for private soldiers. They're allowed ten minutes each and you'd catch something."

"Isn't there an officers' entrance?" asked Hollis. In his innocence he had never contemplated the squalors of vice, and thought only of his simple natural thrill.

"No. You might ask at the chemist's shop. But it may be shut."

"Frost gave me an address that he got from Harrison."

Hollis took his pocket book from his tunic and searched through it. He found the name of the street and the num-ber, and before long they found themselves in the con-ventional and even religious-looking bedroom of a plump woman in her early thirties. She received them like a cheer-ful and hospitable hostess, which made Hollis behave rather as if he were having tea with an archdeacon's wife in Salisbury Close. After ten minutes or so of polite con-versation she became a little brusque and asked if there was anything doing. If not would they please go, and not waste her time. Dominic said: "I will go. My friend would like to stay."

Hollis looked scared, and was about to say that he would go too, but thought that if he did Dominic would despise him. So he stayed to be enveloped in the business-like embrace of this quasi-matron.

Dominic waited for him at the Officers' Club, where Hollis joined him within half an hour. They had a drink together, and without any comment on what had happened they set out for their billets, walking in silence. When they were clear of the town Dominic asked tentatively: "D'you feel better?"

"I took a long time and she got rather cross," Hollis said almost apologetically. They went on in silence, then Dominic said: "I should have dissuaded you."

"Oh, no," said Hollis, sounding resigned and experienced. "One has to learn."

"That is not a thing one should learn. It should be the result of an overpowering impulse."

"I felt pretty impulsive after dinner." They walked another half mile and he added wistfully: "Still, I wish she'd been younger."

They passed the spot where they had sat on the orchard fence.

"I wish I hadn't done it," said Hollis. As he spoke they heard the thin overhead whine of a shell, and the distant crump as it fell on the old houses of Béthune, perhaps, Hollis thought with a dreadful ashamed pity, on the house of the matronly whore.

On the next evening they returned to the front line. The routine was continued, but more lively, or more deathly. One morning from sunrise till noon, a 5·9 shell fell every two minutes on their small sector of the line, more unnerving than a sudden concentrated barrage. Now they returned from the trenches with their ranks more heavily depleted.

The generals ordered more raids to keep the war hot. Towards the end of June the battalion was ordered to carry out one of these. Two platoons were to attack the German trenches, and two to remain guarding their own. Hollis's platoon was detailed to attack, Dominic's to remain. He wanted to go with the attacking party, but Harrison was reluctant to be left with a boy like Hollis as his only subaltern in the event of a counter-attack.

In spite of their strained relations Harrison relied on Dominic to create confidence in the trenches. Frost too was going "over the top".

The raid was to begin at seven o'clock on the evening after they entered the line. At a quarter to seven Dominic came on Hollis in a traverse between their two platoons.

"I hope to God I manage all right," he said. "This sort of thing isn't really my cup of tea." He gave a nervous laugh.

"You'll be all right," said Dominic. "Just go straight ahead but don't walk into our barrage."

Hollis gripped his hand and held it. "Cheerio!" he said and returned to his men.

Dominic stood with sudden melancholy, looking towards the German lines. At the moment the scene could hardly have been more peaceful. The stretch of wasteland before him, where every living growth and every construction of man was blasted and battered flat, suggested the sea at sunset. At this hour in the village churches all over England, they would be singing the last hymn at evensong, where the mothers and lovers of the men huddled nervously in the trenches, waiting for zero hour, had been praying for their safety.

Then, in a second, the heavens opened. Shells crashed on the German lines. Shrapnel burst in golden rain, beautiful in the evening sky. The men straggled out of the trenches across No-man's-land. One of the shells fell short on a section of nine men, killing them all. Now and then a straggling man fell over like a doll, putting his name on a War Memorial. As Dominic watched them, a protective numbness of feeling came over him. He was tense and alert for any need of action on his part. The casualties were not individual human beings – they were only part of the phenomenon.

After some time the raiders returned. Eighty of their number had been killed and more wounded, but they had taken several prisoners and the raid was judged a success. The prisoners were fair round-faced Bavarian peasants, brought back from Russia and bewildered by the fury of the Western Front. The sergeant of Dominic's platoon stood behind a traverse and kicked each one as he passed. Harrison smiled when he heard this, thinking the sergeant "naughty" but amusing.

A platoon was sent out under another barrage to bring in any of the missing wounded. Dominic was in charge of this. They found Hollis with apparently half his face blown away, gurgling and twitching but still alive. Even this did not waken Dominic from his numbness of feeling.

When they came out of the line the surviving officers gave a dinner to celebrate the successful raid. They drank large quantities of champagne, whisky and crème-de-menthe, and they broke the furniture in the *estaminet* where the dinner was held.

One result of all this was that, owing to Hollis and another officer being wounded, and a third killed in the raid, Dominic became due to go on ten days' leave a month sooner than he had expected. He was told of this only the day before his leave began, and he arrived in London without warning.

## CHAPTER SEVEN

WHEN HE LEFT THE TRAIN AT VICTORIA, AND, CARRY-
ing his suitcase, came out into the forecourt of the station,

he again had that feeling of a rarity in the air, of changed laws of gravity, which any sudden return to a once familiar scene gave him. He was surprised to be back so soon, and that his war experience had been so comparatively negligible. He had not been in a great battle, nor seen one German soldier, except the prisoners brought in after the raid. He had seen many killed by shell-fire, and many wounded, but the numbness protected him from the full reality of what he had seen.

Standing uncertainly outside the station he had a feeling of anticlimax, that he was not met by some welcoming face. From childhood, to be welcomed home had seemed to him one of the most important happinesses of life. Once, when a boy, owing to an accident to his foot, he had not been taken on a summer holiday. On the return of the family he had painted a large floral notice, "Welcome Home", and fixed it over the front door. Now, on an occasion which, more than any other, called for joyful faces, there was no one to meet him, and even worse, nowhere he could go except to an hotel.

There was, of course, Sylvia, but when he thought of going to Catherine Street, he had again that slight stoppage in the brain, not a strong or painful one, but enough to keep him standing in indecision. When, in those phases of revulsion from the war, he had sat in some empty traverse, or on the steps of a village church, longing to be back again in the true pattern of human life, it was of Helena whom he thought, of his wife and child on the other side of the world. The week of companionship and that last urgent night with Sylvia had become an incident unrelated to the rest of his life. Her few brief letters and a parcel from Fortnum's had done little to keep it in mind. Yet, unless he went to Cousin Emma, and the thought of this made him feel utterly bleak, he could only go to Sylvia.

He went back through the station into the Grosvenor Hotel, where he booked a room and left his luggage. He then walked along to Catherine Street, but it was more in search of affectionate welcome from someone with whom he had ties of early friendship than to a lovers' meeting.

Just as he rang the bell Sylvia, dressed to go out, opened the door. She started when she saw him, and with the surprise in her eyes was a brief, barely perceptible hostility. Dominic saw it, and expecting a human welcome, a flash of anger came into his own eyes. They were both surprised at this, and Sylvia immediately covered it with an exclamation of delight. She thought it was due on her side to annoyance at his coming without warning. Maurice was shortly due on leave and it would have been awkward if they had met.

"Dominic!" she exclaimed. "Why didn't you let me know that you were coming?"

"I didn't know myself till the last minute. We had some casualties. Hollis was wounded and I went up three places on the leave roll."

"Oh, that was luck. I was just going to tie up parcels, but I'll ring up and say I can't. Come in."

Dominic sat in the miniature grandeur of her drawing-room, while she lied cheerfully to a Miss Charlton on the telephone. He was still dazed by the change of atmosphere, the contrast between this room and the life he had just left. When she put down the telephone she saw that he was not yet with her. Dominic somehow had brought the trenches with him into this exquisite room. Most officers who came on leave washed them away with their first hot bath. What made Dominic so difficult was that he wanted all his worlds to be reconciled, his life integrated. Although so much that he did was instinctive and apparently irrational; in his mind, if frequently smothered by his actions, was that streak of logic, of legal perception, which made his irrational divisions intolerable.

Half an hour later, in Bond Street, he made her more consciously aware of this. He said that he liked walking up Bond Street as it was so different from the trenches. She smiled amiably, but she did not like the remark. She did not like the partitions to be removed between the pigeon-holes of opposing ideas. Necessary inconsistencies should be kept apart so that the pattern of life was not disturbed.

They went into a fashionable tea-shop. An acquaintance of Sylvia's came in, and passing their table, stopped to speak to her. Sylvia introduced Dominic and said that he was an old family friend and just off to stay at Dilton.

"Why did you say that I was going to Dilton?" he asked, when the woman had gone away. "Do you think that I ought to?"

"No, but I thought it better to say that you were."

"Why?"

Sylvia did not answer. She moved the cups on the table and began to pour out the tea. A situation had arisen. She had the same expression as when they walked up the Brompton Road after meeting Cousin Emma, a look of annoyance and uncertainty. Why was he so crude and stupid? It was obvious that she would want to conceal their association. Or was there again no association to conceal?

Dominic hitherto had been so full of his own emotions as a home-coming soldier, that he had not clearly thought of his relationship to Sylvia. He had only been looking for civilization and friendliness. But he was not as stupid as she thought, it was only that his perceptions were stronger than his reasoning facilities. Looking at Sylvia rather petulantly moving the tea-cups, he felt an echo of something else. It was of the woman in Béthune when, after ten minutes of polite conversation, she asked Hollis, if there was nothing doing, to go. He was shocked at himself for thinking of her in connection with that woman, and yet at the same time there was a kind of snap in his brain, as if the jam, the stoppage which so often he felt there, had been finally cleared away, and all that he required of life was open to him.

They did not speak much during tea, but Sylvia's expression of uncertainty faded. They knew that there was an acknowledgement between them. Their bodies were now directing their minds, and there was no need to speak. When they left the tea-shop they took a taxi back to Catherine Street, and sat silent during the short drive. He did not touch her or take her hand. Their feelings were too strong and certain for any trivial caresses.

In her drawing-room she turned to him and they embraced closely, Dominic kissing her hungrily all over her face and neck. They separated, and when she had straightened herself before the grandiose Italian mirror she rang the bell. When her maid came she said: "Mr Langton has just come on leave. He wants a bath."

It was as usual to offer a soldier arriving on leave a bath as a cup of tea, and the maid accepted this customary ritual.

"Will he be staying the night, madam?" she asked.

"No," said Sylvia.

They allowed the maid time to run the bath and put out towels, and then they went upstairs, Sylvia into her own room and Dominic into the bathroom; but when he had undressed he did not get into the bath. He went instead into her room. She had drawn the apricot coloured curtains, on which the sun made a slanting rectangle of light, so that the room was full of a warm evening glow, in which she lay waiting for him on the bed. After months of harsh and squalid living, of brutality and chastity, his passion was almost beyond endurance.

But afterwards he sang in the bath, and when they came down they were more cheerful and easy together than they had ever been. Everything was acknowledged between them. They planned frankly how they could spend his whole leave together, day and night, and decided that it would be best to go out of London.

The snap in his brain, the feeling of mental liberation he had in the tea-shop, had infused his whole body. He had a sense of freedom in his body that filled him with joy. Nothing else mattered. He had won through. All his anxieties, his loneliness and frustrations were wiped away, like dusty webs that had been clouding his sight. He had never known such freedom. Perhaps he had felt a similar joy when he had first been married to Helena, but then it was as if he had entered a haven. He was also taking responsibility. Now he had escaped from enclosing walls and had discarded responsibility. With Helena he was apart from other men. With Sylvia he had broken through into their company. He was the same as other satisfied, normally sensual men, which, he thought, he had always wanted to be. He was full of the delight of his body, and he had ten days of that delight ahead of him. It was enough. All the rest was dreary nonsense. They dined in Sylvia's tiny semi-basement dining-room. The room was so small that it was as if the dugout where he had first dined in the front line had been touched by some golden fairy's wand. Sylvia again wore a dress of stiff yellow silk, and in the shaded light of the candles looked as if she were a portrait in the room. Her face was softened not only by this light, but by Dominic's passionate love-making, so that it had a look of having undergone suffering, of a sad wisdom, mellowing her chiselled perfection.

When they came up into the brighter light of the drawing-room this illusion faded. They were lively and cheerful together, furthering the conspiracy of their bodies.

Sylvia had brought out a large map of England. They spread it on the floor and knelt beside it, looking for some place where they could go to stay. Sylvia, who had a wide acquaintance in the English counties, ruled out areas where they might run into her friends. Dominic, his romanticism working automatically, suggested Cornwall.

"It's a long way to go," she said, "but perhaps that's a good thing. What part of Cornwall?"

"Penzance," said Dominic.

"Why Penzance?"

"I like the name," he said.

She laughed and rang up Paddington station to ask about the trains. The best one left at ten in the morning.

"We can't catch that – not tomorrow," she said as she put down the telephone.

"Why not?" asked Dominic.

"It's only twelve hours from now. I shall have to make all kinds of arrangements and everyone will be asleep."

"Look," he said. "I've only got ten days' leave. I can't waste one."

"No. But I can't leave London till after tomorrow."

"You could if it was a matter of life and death."

"I suppose so."

"Well, pretend it is. It is to me – a matter of life."

"Very well. I will," she said. "I must telephone like blazes."

First of all she rang up two or three London friends and put off social engagements. Then she rang up Hermione Maine, a friend who lived in Hertfordshire, where she had turned her country house into a hospital for convalescent officers. She asked her if she would say that she was staying there, if there were any enquiries for her in the next week. She would telephone her real address. She then wrote brief notes to Miss Charlton and to her mother, saying that Hermione wanted her to go down and help her at the hospital for a few days. All these deceptions, which normally would have disgusted Dominic, he accepted as necessary to remove the obstacles between him and his strong desire.

"There," said Sylvia, as she stamped the letter to her mother. "Now, I've only got to tell the servants that I'm going down to Hermione's in the morning."

"You can do anything if you want to do it strongly enough," said Dominic.

"Have you always done what you wanted?" asked Sylvia a little quizzically.

"Not always. But I'm going to from now on," he said.

As he walked back to his hotel, having arranged to meet her at Paddington in the morning, he felt that he could always do what he wanted. It was easy he thought, when you knew what you wanted, and he certainly knew that. Hitherto his mind had been confused with childish scruples and nonsense.

In the morning while he was dressing, the telephone rang in his room. It was Sylvia. She had not taken into account the fact that through travelling so often with her father down to Frome, she was well known at Paddington station. She said that it would be better if they did not meet openly on the platform, but entered the train separately, joining each other after it had started. Dominic agreed to this reluctantly. In his new sense of power and freedom he did not want to have to take into account the moral susceptibilities of railway porters.

Followed by one of them he walked along the platform where the Cornish express was waiting, and had a glimpse of Sylvia already installed in an otherwise empty compartment. She had given a good tip to keep it so, and the porter was used to obliging her father in the same way.

As soon as the train had started Dominic moved along to join her. Apart from this arrangement, and the fact that when the train an hour or two later whizzed through Frome Sylvia pulled down the blind by her window, there was no suggestion of romance about their escapade. They were like two friends who had planned a holiday together, or even like a married couple returning to the country after a London visit. After luncheon in the dining-car they returned to doze in their compartment, or browsed through the illustrated papers which Sylvia had bought, until they arrived at Penzance late in the afternoon.

They went to the largest and presumably the best hotel, where they booked a room and a dressing-room as man and wife. The rooms were large and darkly furnished, but the hotel was high up, and the windows looked across the bay to St Michael's Mount. The evening sun, shining on the little monastery-castle which crowned the mount, made it appear like some Wagnerian shrine of the Holy Grail. While Sylvia was changing after her journey, Dominic leaned on his window-sill and stared across at it. He liked seeing famous places of which he had heard in his childhood. He was pleased that they could see it from their windows. Without it these hotel rooms might have been a little sordid.

At dinner they became more cheerful and conscious of the object of their journey. The food down here was better than that in London restaurants, and they had good wine. Afterwards they walked for half an hour or so on the darkened quay, but Dominic was impatient to return to the hotel. It may have been because of the provincial dullness, the heavy respectability of their rooms, that he put out the lights when he came into her room. He did not want to feast his eyes on her in this place, but he flung open the window to the summer night and the stars, the sea and the castle.

His love-making was not as burning but it was as strong as the evening before. They lay locked together, believing that they were at last one, each possessing the other, finally, absolutely for eternity.

But when in the morning, after they had parted to dress, they met again to go down to breakfast, it was as if a curtain had fallen between them. Afterwards they walked about the town, looking at the old houses and into the shop windows. But something had gone from their daytime relationship, the tension, the bickering which indicated exciting possibilities. The possibilities had become certainties, and for the moment that gave them a deeper satisfaction, but it made it harder to pass the time. In the afternoon they hired a motor-car and drove to Land's End.

On the second night he was less urgent in his love-making. It was as if he wondered after all whether he really knew her, and was trying to understand her so that she would be truly his own. He was like a blind man trying to learn her with his hands. It seemed that he could never satisfy this curiosity to know her, could never understand what he was seeking in her.

In the small hours of the morning he awoke and saw a waning moon in the square of the window. He left the bed and went to look out at the castle on its little island across the bay, now more remote and mysterious, more legendary than ever in the moonlight. He wanted to understand it in the same way that he wanted to understand Sylvia, to know why it filled him with longing to be united to something outside himself.

She awoke and found he was not beside her. Then she saw him by the window, his bare shoulders outlined by the moonlight.

[92]

"What are you doing?" she asked, and came over to join him. He thought that she was sharing his feeling about the castle and the sea. He felt her arm against his own, and he turned and drew her to him, wanting to make her share his feeling about the castle and the sea, to extend his love to include every beautiful thing.

The next morning again the curtain descended between them. They walked about the town almost in boredom. Dominic reminded himself that it was marvellous for him to be walking in this peaceful sleepy town.

"It's wonderful to be out of the trenches," he said.

"Yes. It must be," said Sylvia, but for her it was only an intellectual idea. In the afternoon he wanted to go over to St Michael's Mount, but Sylvia did not like going over country houses as a sightseer. She thought it was like prying on people whom later she might meet. There was even the possibility that there might be someone staying there who knew her by sight. She seemed to be daily more anxious about the risks of their escapade.

When they awoke next morning they followed the same routine, the descending curtain of convention, the breakfast, the newspapers, the stroll, the shops.

In the afternoon they went to St Ives. Dominic suggested dining there and returning afterwards to Penzance. She thought that would be tiresome. Then she said: "Oh, very well." At least it would give them something to talk about.

On this night Dominic stood a long time at the window, looking at the sea and the castle, which she refused to visit. She became impatient, not because she was urgent to have him beside her, but because a kind of remoteness in his attitude irritated her.

In the morning Sylvia woke him early and said that she wanted to leave Penzance. She felt that she could not bear another morning looking in the same shop windows.

"Where can we go?" asked Dominic, sleepy and bemused.

"Why not return to London? There's always something to do, and it's really safer. We're rather conspicuous here." This was certainly true. With the contrast in their good looks, with Sylvia's quiet air of wealth and unconscious arrogance, they were splendid exotic animals in the provincial street – a black and a golden panther.

Dominic ran his hands through his hair. He thought that in some way he had failed her, as he had failed himself. On that first evening at Catherine Street he had imagined that the delight in his body, that wild sense of power – it was not free love that he had enjoyed but wild love – was enough in itself, that it had banished forever all his doubts and uncertain aspirations. But he could not change his nature in a night, and he still expected that in Cornwall his love would have some meaning beyond itself, would be linked up with the moonlit castle and the sea.

Sylvia had no idea that this was his expectation. She knew perfectly well what she wanted. She wanted him physically. She wanted to experience his passionate unrestrained love-making without fear of interruption by her maid. She knew her own mind, and was confident that as the daughter of a rich peer, every idea she held was the right one. She was sure she was entitled to the best, and as Dominic's bodily passion was like a flame consuming her, whereas Maurice's was matter of fact and correct like all his other activities, and as she thought Maurice lucky to have married her and therefore in no position to complain, she really believed that it was right and natural that she should have Dominic if she wanted him. It was her *droit de la grande dame*. But she did not think that her feelings for Dominic or his for her had any point beyond their own physical satisfaction.

Because he thought he had failed her he agreed to go. Sylvia then said that if they hurried they could catch the morning train, and they left Penzance as impulsively as they had come there.

At breakfast she put forward another plan to him, that he should leave the express at Exeter and go on by a slow train to Frome, and spend a night or two at Dilton with her parents. She had various motives for this. One was that it would avoid the risk of his being seen with her at Paddington. Also, it would put out of her mother's mind any idea that they had been together. Most of all perhaps because she would not mind a few days' rest from his exclusive company. She told him what she knew would convince him, but what she also believed, that her father would be hurt if he did not go to see them.

"Shouldn't I let them know?" asked Dominic doubtfully.

"You can ring up from the station," said Sylvia. "On leave you can do anything. Anyhow, they'll be delighted to see you. Say you've been to stay with a friend in Cornwall. They think I'm with Hermione."

When he left her in the train at Exeter they kissed in a rather perfunctory way, but comfortable and friendly.

"You'd better stay two days with the family," she said. "I'll go to Hermione for tonight. Ring up when you get to London."

It was all matter of fact, and from Sylvia's point of view entirely satisfactory. Dominic thought too that perhaps it was better this way than if they were in such an emotionally heightened condition that they could not bear to part for a minute, the condition he was in when he left Helena.

He rang up from the Frome railway station and Lady Dilton said that they would be delighted to see him, and that she would send a car for him at once.

When he arrived she was still engaged in sending out

some kind of circular or charity invitation, and she gave the impression that she had not left her writing table since he last saw her.

"I hope you didn't mind my coming without warning," said Dominic, and blurted out: "Sylvia said I might come."

"Of course not." She gave him a sharp glance. "You've seen Sylvia?"

"Yes. I saw her in London," said Dominic, a little awkward and hesitating, but he was often like this when sharply questioned.

"I rang up last night and they said she was in Hertfordshire."

"I saw her the day I arrived," explained Dominic, more confidently. "I've been in Cornwall for a few days."

"Have you friends there?" asked Lady Dilton, but without interest. She went on to say that her husband would be over to dinner and would "want to hear all about the war".

When Lord Dilton arrived he was delighted to see Dominic, for every reason – personally because he liked him; also because he heard he had done well at the front and so had brought credit to the territorial battalion, justifying his confidence in the ugly duckling; and also because he was touched that a young man on leave should be so thoughtful as to desert the gaieties of London to come to stay with two old fogies. He immediately went down to the cellars to find something worthy of him.

At dinner he made his old jokes about the bath water, and Dominic had a contented and peaceful feeling of being at home. His simplicity made him accept odd situations, until he was aware of considerations which showed them to be outrageous. It did not occur to him that it was shocking, even treacherous, to accept the affection and confidence of people whose married daughter he had seduced, and whom he had parted from only a few hours earlier. It was partly because he regarded the Tunstalls as a group, responsible for each other. In times past they had presented themselves as a group, rather an overbearing one. When he was engaged to Sylvia he had the sense of being engaged to all the Tunstalls. So now because Sylvia, who bossed her parents, had told him to come here, he thought it quite allowable to do so; and he almost felt that her parents must know and approve the liaison. Anyhow it could hardly be called a seduction.

When Lord Dilton heard that Dominic was staying for two days, he said that he would come over again to dine on the following evening. "Or would you like to dine in the mess?" he asked. Dominic said apologetically that when he was on leave it was more of a treat for him to dine in a private house.

"Can't you find some young people to make it a bit cheerful for him?" Lord Dilton asked his wife.

"I like it here just as it is," said Dominic.

"I can ask Marcus," said Lady Dilton.

"That'll be lively," said Lord Dilton.

Colonel Rodgers, frustrated by his failure at the War Office, had become the incarnation of a small war in himself. There was anger in every movement, in every tone of his staccato voice. In his tight old-fashioned dinner jacket he looked more than ever like a large ant. During the whole of dinner he was angry, about the larger strategy of the war, and about subalterns who took the stiffening out of their army caps and wore pale yellow collars. At the suggestion that the war might end before long he actually trembled with anger, although he drank only water, following the strangely nonconformist example of the King; while his brother-in-law and Dominic finished the decanter of burgundy between them.

When Lady Dilton had left the room he questioned

4 + W.B.S.

Dominic about every detail of life in the trenches, and even asked him if he had "killed his man". Lord Dilton was fidgety and bored. When he passed round the port Colonel Rodgers pushed it on impatiently. Nothing mellow or pleasant must interrupt the steely stark horror which was his obsession. Everything must be hell. Dominic, relaxed after four nights of desperate love-making, felt himself defenceless against the violence of the colonel's mania.

Lord Dilton pushed back his chair abruptly and said: "We'd better go in to Edith. She'll want a rubber before you go." He did not wait to blow out the candles as was his usual custom.

The rubber of bridge was more distracting than the dinner. During every deal, and even when he was dummy, Colonel Rodgers continued questioning Dominic about the trenches. When Lord Dilton was dummy he pulled the bell-rope, and asked for the whisky tray immediately, hoping it would speed his brother-in-law's departure. As soon as the rubber was finished, the colonel, with superfluous apologies for leaving early, said that he must go. When he said goodbye to Dominic his angry voice warmed a little with emotion, and in his strange insect's eyes was a ray of affection.

As soon as he had gone Lady Dilton said fretfully: "I wish Marcus would attend to his cards." She went up to bed.

"Well, that was a cheerful evening," said Lord Dilton. "I'm sorry." He began to pour out whisky, and said: "Say when."

They sat down in armchairs, and he suddenly exclaimed: "Marcus is mad. He thinks the war is to give him an interest in his old age. He doesn't know or care where it's leading as long as it doesn't stop. I wish I knew myself." He drank some of his whisky, and asked: "What do you think?"

Dominic had never thought where the war was leading, nor had any of the men in his regiment. They concerned themselves with their immediate duties, and had a vague idea that afterwards there would be an earthly paradise for those heroes who had not gone to a heavenly one.

"There you are," said Lord Dilton. "If the soldiers at the front have no idea of what they are up to, who has? It seems to me that the cost of moving the trenches one way or the other is out of all proportion to the advantage gained, if there is any advantage in owning an extra bit of blasted heath. D'you think there is any chance of getting them really on the run this year?"

"I'm afraid I don't know, sir," said Dominic.

Lord Dilton looked moodily at his whisky. His conscience was beginning to trouble him. It was further disturbed by Marcus's repulsive conversation. For three years he had been training subalterns and after a few months sending them out to France, into the Moloch jaws. After another few months they were either dead, those decent boys, or back again wounded, and there was no result for all this, or any sign of a result. The line scarcely wavered.

"I thought you went to war to get some advantage out of it," he said. "We seem to be going to war to ruin ourselves. I don't like the Germans much. The Kaiser's a pompous ass, but I'm not prepared to commit suicide out of spite: and I'd rather have a German general than that damned Welsh Baptist. What the devil has the 'sword of the Lord and Gideon' got to do with the Prime Minister of England? He wants a 'knock-out blow' and he'll knock out Europe, England included. He hates us. He declared war on us long ago." By "us" Lord Dilton meant the landowners.

"Now he has found an easy way to wipe us out," he went on. "Look at the Wolverhamptons. Old Wolverhampton died. They had to pay death duties. A week later his eldest son, 'the first of the litter', was killed. The second son was killed a month ago – a third lot of death duties. The family exterminated and the estate confiscated, the reward for serving your country. What's left goes to the daughter who has married the son of one of those damned newspaper peers who are hounding us on to ruin. When you pretend you're waging war from high moral principles, you're on the way to hell. You've taken off the brakes. The war is really to make fortunes for the men who are going to buy our confiscated estates. Lansdowne is the only one with the guts to point it out, and they all attack him, and say we're not going to stop the war to preserve Lansdowne House and Bowood. What sort of country will this be when Bowoods are gone, and the Diltons and Waterparks too? I always thought that England was the Bowoods and the Diltons and the Waterparks, with the farms and cottages around them."

His eyes in his heavy red kind face stared in angry questioning at Dominic, who did not know what to answer. He had thought that he was fighting to save Waterpark and his farm in Australia from being seized by the Kaiser, not to lose them.

"Perhaps I should not talk to you like this," said Lord Dilton, becoming suddenly diffident. "You're a serving soldier. But I feel that I have a responsibility that I'm avoiding, and there are not many people I can talk to freely. You have always seemed to me honest in your opinions. But you'd better forget it."

He poured himself out another whisky "for the road" and drank it quickly. Dominic went with him to his car which was waiting at a side door. There they shook hands warmly.

"It was good of you to come down," said Lord Dilton. "The best of luck. You mustn't take what I said too seriously."

As he drove away he wondered if he would ever see Dominic again, whether he would be dead in a month. He wondered about his own sons, if they too would go before long, and his family would suffer the fate of Wolverhampton's.

In the morning Dominic lay in that pale green bath in which he had first thought of Sylvia. He could see through the low-silled window into the park, where the still, drowsy morning promised a hot day. The shadow of an oak tree was like a pool on the grass in which some of Lord Dilton's famous black cattle were munching and whisking their tails.

He felt that he had broken through to an extension of experience since he had lain here imagining Sylvia. His imagination had passed into knowledge. Also Lord Dilton's comments on the war had influenced him more than he knew, and more than Lord Dilton would have wished. They increased his feeling that reality differed from his imagination, and that he was beginning to know it, that he was becoming adult in his mind as well as his body. Cracks were appearing in the darkness which had surrounded him all his life, and gleams of light were coming through.

When he left later in the morning, Lady Dilton came out to the car with him, and to his surprise she kissed him as she said goodbye. It still did not occur to him that he should not accept all their kindness and affection, coming straight from his escapade with Sylvia.

On arriving in London he went to the little Mayfair hotel and rang her up, but was told that she was out at luncheon. She would be back later in the afternoon. He knew that he should go to see Cousin Emma while he was on leave, and he took this opportunity.

It was still early when he arrived at Brompton Square, and she was just coming down from her rest. She was extremely fragile, and needed to cherish herself carefully if she was to keep the flag flying. The unexpectedness of his visit jolted her slightly. She implied a rebuke that half past three was not a fashionable hour at which to call, but said that she was glad to see him. He thanked her for the plum cake. She asked him if he was going to Dilton, and he said that he had just come from there.

"Did you see that pretty girl you were engaged to?" she asked. "The one you introduced to me outside the Oratory?"

"She wasn't there," said Dominic.

"It's a pity you didn't marry her," said Cousin Emma, with the insolence of an old woman who has lived for "society".

She had thrown a stone into the pond of Dominic's emotions. His pride and his love for Helena were immediately affronted; but at the same time her remark stimulated his desire for Sylvia. The two things were in sudden violent conflict. He looked bewildered and furious.

He wanted to leave the house as soon as possible. He felt suffocated in the stuffy Edwardian drawing-room, over-crowded and tasteless, with some beautiful old English furniture cluttered up with Second Empire rubbish. He even was repelled by Cousin Emma's stuffy festive old lady's clothes, so much jewellery and feathers and black lace. His repudiation of her and her whole way of life was an unconscious attempt to reconcile Helena and Sylvia in his own mind. They both wanted what was fresh, passion-ate and alive. He did not realize that Sylvia in the course of time would become a latter-day Cousin Emma; nor that Cousin Emma had once been a late Victorian Sylvia.

He soon stood up to leave, and she became once more a kind, affectionate old lady, promising another plum cake. He thanked her but said that things were hotting up in France, and the delivery of parcels would be uncertain.

When he was walking the short distance from the door to the Brompton Road, he had a feeling that made him look back. He saw that she was standing on one of the little iron first-floor balconies, waving to him. He was filled with discomfort and sadness, and again it seemed an extension of knowledge. That day, of the two hardest, most socially inexorable women he knew, one had impulsively kissed him goodbye; the other stood, regardless of the sedate conventions of the square, waving to him from the balcony. She nodded her head and he could see some little stiff black flowers quivering in her bonnet.

He walked to the top of Sloane Street and took a bus to Victoria. Sylvia tried to impress on him that if he must use a public conveyance he should take a taxi, not a bus, but he would not spend any money on himself which could be sent to Helena. So now, though he was going to see Sylvia, he went in a way that was going to save money for his wife.

She was not yet at home and he went in to wait for her. She came in a few minutes later, and seemed a little startled to find him there, reading an evening paper which her maid had given him. He looked so well established, as if he belonged to the place.

"Have you brought your luggage?" she asked, and was relieved when he said that it was at the hotel. This was partly because she did not want him to appear too naturally at home here, but also because she intended to ask him to stay on the following night, his last of leave, when he had the excuse of the early train.

The conspiracy between them had now become open. They argued about it. She suggested dining in a restaurant. Dominic wanted to dine in.

"If we dine at a restaurant will you come to the hotel afterwards?" he asked.

"No. That would be much too risky."

"It's risky here.".

"Not when you're staying. Tomorrow." She kissed him and they laughed.

The following evening, as on the previous occasion, they came in early to dinner and did not go out again. She suggested that he might like to go to a play on his last night, but he only said: "What for?"

Throughout the night they made love greedily, seeking nothing but physical satisfaction, taking all the pleasure they could in each other while it was accessible.

In the morning again she went with him to Victoria, and as before Dominic met there a subaltern whom he knew, not one of his regiment, but a young man whom he had met on a Lewis-gun course. Despondent that his leave was over, the subaltern was pleased to find a companion with whom he could travel back to France. Thinking, as Hollis had done, that Sylvia was Dominic's wife, and without sufficient imagination to realize that if this were so they would not want to spend their last minutes together gossiping with a stranger, he attached himself to them. Sylvia turned on him and asked coldly: "Have you been over the top yet?"

"Not exactly," said the subaltern, and looking hurt and confused he drifted away.

Dominic quickly shut this incident out of his mind. He felt the symptoms of an inner explosion which he could not possibly allow at this moment. He thought hard of the wonderful time Sylvia had given him, and when he had to enter the train he tried to express his thanks; but he used more the language suitable to a hostess, than that from a lover torn away by a war.

In the train he felt an uneasiness in his mind, but soon he fell asleep, and did not wake up till Folkestone. Through all the bustle of embarkation, during the crossing, and when he landed at Boulogne, he was conscious of this uneasiness, that there was something in his mind that he would not face. He was told that he had to catch a train at half past seven for Béthune. He went to the Officers' Club, and sat there dozing in an armchair. Sometimes he ordered a drink and then fell asleep. When he slept the curves and creases round his mouth were heavy and voluptuous. His black silky hair fell over his forehead, and he was dark under the eyes. One or two of the officers looked at him curiously, and no one cared to speak to him.

At last it was time to go to the train. When it jolted, rattled and crawled out of Boulogne station, it was like a suitable transport to hell. The windows were broken, the seats stained with rain and spilt beer, the woodwork was cut and scribbled with obscenities. The two other officers in the carriage lighted candles and stuck them guttering on the window ledge. They sat opposite each other at the far end of the carriage. They said good evening to Dominic when he came in, but they had been to the same school and spoke exclusively to each other. One was a staff captain. Dominic heard him say: "They're trying to create a tradition of fair play between the Hun airman and our own. We've got to stop that. The only good Boche is a dead one."

Dominic felt the symptoms of an explosion again. He could not control it. It burst and he said violently: "Damn you, shut up!"

The staff captain turned to him with the manner of a prefect to whom a small boy has been rude, but when he saw Dominic's blazing eyes he really thought that he was in a carriage with a madman, and he said nothing. Soon afterwards the crawling train stopped at a wayside station. The staff captain and his friend took their luggage from the rack, their candles from the window ledge and moved to another carriage.

4*

Dominic sat alone in the darkness. The explosion had been like the bursting of some inner growth, spreading poison through his body. All kinds of black imaginings rose into his mind, affecting his thoughts about Sylvia. The staff captain's remark about the airmen was somehow linked up with her brutal question to the subaltern at Victoria Station. She and the staff captain were the same type. Why had she asked the subaltern how much danger he had known? How dared she from her life of safety and pleasure? How dared the staff captain, safe in some château behind the line, tell the airmen that they should abandon their decencies?

He began to have horrible suspicions about her. He remembered the competence with which she arranged their times together, the ready lies she told, the ease with which she took him. Had she brought out that map of England for other men? Were certain areas ruled out, not because she knew the local families, but because she had already been there with someone else?

Then he thought of himself and his suspicions as contemptible. She had given him a wonderful time. His head began to ache with conflicting ideas. He was exhausted. She had drained the life out of him. But he had worshipped the beauty of her body. Yet last night she had only drained the life out of him. It was a night of pure sensuality, without love, without meaning. Their bodies had acted with practised skill to achieve the extreme pleasure. There was no tenderness between them.

He fell asleep again and had confused and odd dreams. He knew that there was violence in his nature, and that it was said to be inherited from a Spaniard who had strangled altar boys in the crypts of his castle, the ancestor who was a joke to his brothers. To Dominic he was no joke, but a horror latent in his blood. In his dream he was still hearing the staff captain talking, though he had left the carriage. He also was somehow Harrison and also Colonel Rodgers. He was saying: "We must have the orgasm, the orgasm of killing. Never mind women. Pierce another man with a sword. Don't release the seed of life, but the blood of death."

Dominic woke up with a jolt, sweating and nauseated. He believed that he had met the evil in himself face to face, and he was afraid to go to sleep again.

## CHAPTER EIGHT

WHEN AT LAST IN THE EARLY DAWN THE CRAWLING train reached Béthune, he learned that the battalion was out of the line at a village some kilometres away. He went to the Hôtel de France to have a bath and breakfast, and then to the Officers' Club, where he hung about trying to get transport to the battalion, which he did not reach until late in the afternoon. He was directed to his company mess, in one of the inevitable peasants' cottages. It was deserted except for his servant, who took him to his billet and gave him some letters. Finch, the servant, was a youth of about nineteen, modest, intelligent, with sensitive manners which put some of the public school subalterns to shame. As they walked to the billet in another peasant's cottage, he told Dominic the battalion gossip, that it was said they were going to take part in a big attack soon.

The letters had been forwarded from his Australian bank in London. He could have had them when he was on leave but he had not called there, as it was out of his way. He had cashed cheques at Cox's, the army bank, or at the hotel. Amongst the letters was one from Helena. He glanced through the others and took Helena's out into a meadow behind the cottage. Here it was very peaceful. There was a little stream bordered with pollarded willows, and a row of taller trees made long shadows across the grass. He thought that in this quiet place her letter could heal him. She had always been able to dispel his evil spirits. A hideous dream, like that in the train, could not happen when she was sleeping by his side. She was his life and his health. As he took out her letter into the peaceful meadow he was not troubled by his infidelity with Sylvia, as he had never thought of her as a substitute for Helena. He had no feelings of uneasiness, as sitting on the grass by the stream he opened her letter, only the hope of his restoration.

She was ill in bed, she wrote, with some disease she had caught while dipping the sheep. She repeated that she had to do this because she had dismissed Harry who would not go to the war. She was in the hospital in the nearest town, but she expected to return to the farm in a week. She had no other news.

This letter, instead of bringing Dominic peace, churned up more conflicting feelings in him, the first an awful pity for Helena lying in bed with a disease caught from animals. The Calvinism he had been taught by his governess in his childhood at last bore on his relations with Sylvia. He felt that he had brought the disease, a divine retribution on Helena, part of the mad vindictive "justice" which he had been taught was an attribute of God. At the same time he had a recurrence of his anger with her for dismissing Harry, now more disturbing as he linked it up with Sylvia's question to the subaltern on Victoria Station, and the staff captain's comments on the chivalrous airmen. Why should the Hollises and the Harrys go on pouring out their blood in the trenches for Sylvia's pleasures and the staff captain's promotion, or even for Helena's safety? The hatred of the old, even of people as old as himself, rose up in him again. He thrust Helena's letter into his pocket, and feeling on edge with everything, he went along to the company mess. He found Frost there, and a new subaltern called Raife.

Harrison also had just returned from leave, three days in Paris. His bedroom opened off the room used as the mess. He was changing and when he heard voices he came in and sat on the floor in his underclothes. He was a little drunk and very pleased with himself. He drank more as he told them of his exploits. He had gone to an expensive brothel and picked one from a choice of girls. He showed them her photograph. She was rather like himself, fair, with a narrow forehead and a beaky nose. They had spent three days and nights together. He described them in detail. It had cost him fifty pounds.

Finch and another officer's servant came in and out of the room during this recital. They were laying the table for dinner. They had faintly uncomfortable silly smiles on their faces. Dominic hated to see them degraded by this half-deference to Harrison's squalor.

Raiffe lifted a glass filled with Cointreau and white wine. "Here's to the three F's!" he exclaimed. They stood for war, hunting and sex.

Harrison was so pleased with himself that he tried to make a gesture of reconciliation towards Dominic.

"I bet you've been having some fun too, Langton," he said. "Come on, tell us all about it, you sly old bastard."

The turmoil in Dominic became unbearable. He demanded that there should be a difference between his feelings for Sylvia and Harrison's for the whore in Paris, but he could find none. To be completely honest he should be sitting drunk and half-naked on the floor, shouting about the three F's. This further conflict in his mind, added to what he had felt in the train, and the effect of Helena's letter filled him with a new explosive violence. A spark was put to it by Harrison's use of the word "bastard".

Dominic's mind was full of antique conventions, which were the cause of much of his unconventionality. He firmly believed that anyone who had been called a bastard could not honourably survive unless he had drawn the other man's blood. He believed that Harrison had stated that his mother, in whom for him were gathered all kindness and human dignity, was no better than the woman he had bought in Paris. He knew that if he attempted to speak he would only stutter inarticulately. His eyes blazed but the flesh sagged on his face so that it looked like a skull. He pushed back his chair, knocking it over, and he left the room. The other three officers were momentarily sobered, and Raife asked: "What's he up to?"

Dominic went back to his billet where he wrote a note to Jackson, a subaltern in C Company. He said that Harrison had grossly insulted him, and that he was going to challenge him to a duel. Would Jackson act as his second? Jackson had a French mother and both his parents lived in Paris. He was not a close friend of Dominic's but on the few occasions when they had spoken together there had seemed to be a sympathy of ideas between them. His conventions, like Dominic's, were more medieval than public school.

When Dominic had written his note, Finch arrived to tell him that dinner was ready. Dominic said that he was not coming to dinner and told Finch to take the note to Jackson, who, however, was not as medieval as himself.

Jackson thought it fantastic for a lieutenant to challenge his company commander, or in fact anyone else to a duel. If either of them were wounded, or even if it became known without this, there would be a terrific shindy. Dominic might be court-martialled, or even shot for wounding a superior officer in (technically) the field, and he would be a party to it. He sympathized with Dominic's attitude, but he was extremely worried. He told Finch that there was no answer, and he went round to A Company mess to see Harrison, who was at dinner.

"Good evening," he said. "Langton wants to shoot you."

Raife grinned, Frost looked concerned, and Harrison went white. He thought Dominic quite capable of shooting him.

"What do you mean?" he asked, though he understood that Jackson had come in the capacity of a second.

"He says that you called him a bastard." Jackson, although he wanted to prevent a duel, also wanted Harrison to suffer the apprehension of one.

"It was only a joke."

"Langton doesn't take it that way. He doesn't think a gentleman calls another a bastard, even as a joke."

"Is Langton a gentleman? I thought he was an Australian," said Harrison.

"Shall I tell him that? If so you'd better say your prayers," Jackson replied, himself now touchy that his friend was further insulted.

Harrison tried to laugh as if the whole thing were childish.

"Well, what's the programme?" he asked.

"I only have a note from him. I haven't seen him yet. I suppose that you choose your weapons. . . . But you're in for a hell of a row whatever happens. If Langton wounds you there'll be a court martial. If on the other hand it comes out that you called one of your junior officers a bastard and then shot him, it won't help your career."

"It's all mad," said Harrison irritably. "What d'you want me to do?"

"You could apologize."

Harrison looked sullen, but at last said: "Very well."

"Shall I tell him that?" asked Jackson. "You'd better come with me."

Harrison went into his room to put on his Sam Browne and a cap and they walked round to Dominic's billet. Jackson told him to wait outside.

Dominic was sitting at a table trying to write a letter of instructions to a family lawyer in Melbourne about certain dispositions in the event of his death.

"Have you told him?" he asked Jackson as he came in.

"I've spoken to him. He's willing to apologize."

"I didn't ask him to apologize. I sent him a challenge," said Dominic smouldering.

"It makes things a bit awkward," said Jackson.

"I'm used to awkwardness," Dominic retorted. "It's my constant companion. Did you give him my challenge?"

"I told him about it."

"What did he say?"

"He said he would apologize."

"I don't want an apology. He sat there wallowing half-naked and drunk on the floor, with the men laying the table." A curious old-maidish primness came into his voice, grotesque in the context. "And then he insulted my mother."

"That wasn't his intention. You see he's not a gentleman." It gave Jackson a malicious pleasure to say this. He also thought, understanding Dominic's medieval mind, that it might make him less anxious to fight Harrison. It seemed to have an effect on him.

Jackson followed up his advantage. He pointed out the possible repercussions of a duel, the harm not only to Dominic or to Harrison, but to their relatives and to the regiment. "After all," he said, "you want to keep your bullets for the real enemy."

As he spoke Dominic seemed to go away from him, to retreat into his private gloom. When he spoke his voice changed, and had become oddly remote.

"Harrison is my real enemy," he said. "The Germans are only my artificial enemy. I know nothing about them except what I read in the papers. When I see them, when the prisoners come in, they are not my enemies. They are the same as everyone else. They are just like the people you see in the street – in London or Melbourne or Paris or any-where. They are not my real enemies. Harrison is my real enemy."

Jackson was puzzled. "He's waiting outside to apolo-gize," he said.

"All right. Let him come in," said Dominic indifferently.

Jackson went to the door and signed to Harrison, who came in half-sheepishly, half-hearty. He spoke to Dominic in a slightly patronizing way, as if he had been stupid to take seriously anything said so lightly. He offered his hand. Dominic held out his own, but his clasp was lifeless.

"Now let's go back to dinner," said Harrison. "Will you come with us?" he asked Jackson.

Dominic said: "I must finish my letter," and the other two thought it best to leave him.

He sat down again and stared at his unfinished letter. It had no meaning for him and he tore it up. He felt a deathly exhaustion. Both his mind and his body refused to function any more, and he lay down on the bed. After the conflicts inside him, followed by the violent currents of rage against Harrison, all his fuses were burnt out. Finch came in and found him lying asleep in his clothes, with the lights on. He woke him, and Dominic let him help him undress and get into bed.

He fell asleep at half past eight, and except for the semi-conscious five minutes while Finch put him to bed, he slept deeply and dreamlessly for eleven hours. He no longer attempted to resolve his inner conflicts. He followed his routine duties mechanically, and sat silent at meals. Except for Raife, who liked anything or anyone who increased the tension and colour of life, he was treated with mistrust. Harrison and Frost were a little afraid of him.

He had always had the idea that authority was right, and his troubles had largely come from his attempts to reconcile his own ideas of virtue with the rightness he expected to find in authority. Now after the conflict in his mind which lasted from his parting with Sylvia at Victoria until his failure to provoke Harrison to a duel, he no longer made the attempt. A kind of savage humility had come upon him. The violence in him which he had always felt was his most evil trait, revealed so clearly in his dream in the train, was now endorsed by authority; and as it happened with a new emphasis.

The governments and the generals on both sides must at this time have been on tenterhooks lest the soldiers woke up to the suicidal futility of their lives, that some common humanity such as that of Christmas 1914, or the sheer weariness which the French were beginning to show, might lead them simply to stop fighting. It would have been a disaster for either High Command if the enemy had walked away. There would have been no glory attached to victory. At Christmas 1914, this disaster had been prevented by a high-ranking English officer firing into the German lines while the opposing troops were dancing together round bonfires in No-man's-land. At Etaples there had been a riot and the soldiers had killed five military policemen. Always there was fear of the psychological uncertainty of a million men, and everything possible was done to prevent peace breaking out. Lloyd George addressed those Old Testament exhortations to the armies, which so disgusted Lord Dilton. He would not consider an armistice "as it might be difficult to get the nations fighting again". Raids like that in which Hollis was wounded were ordered "to keep alive the spirit of offensive". A general came to inspect the battalion. He asked each subaltern: "What were you in civilian life?" When the young man answered modestly: "I was at school," or "I was reading law," the general replied: "Well, you're going to be a soldier for the rest of your life, remember that." And this was true for a number of them, as half the battalion was wiped out in the approaching attack, though the general ended his days playing golf in Surrey.

Now authority in its nervousness sent out orders that officers were to give their men lectures on the physical pleasures of fighting, of the orgasm of killing, of which Dominic had dreamed in the train. Each subaltern was told to take his platoon into a barn and give them this harangue. It was rather like giving them a talk on "the facts of life". Everyone was embarrassed. Even Raife, with this opportunity to elaborate the theme of his three F's, could only say: "Well we're here to fight and we've jolly well got to do it. Anyone who doesn't know how had better ask the sergeant-major." Frost recited Kipling's "If" to his platoon.

To Dominic alone this instruction was poison. If authority endorsed the evil that was in him, at last he would be obedient. He could, as it were, say "evil be thou my good" with a clear conscience. Returning from exhaustion, with an empty heart and mind he took violence as his god, and in this spirit he addressed his men. He was also the son of artists and was able to recreate his feelings in his imagination. When he spoke of the pleasure of killing another man, his words had the strength and impact of a work of art. He did not merely give them a few facts to which they could listen in half-hearted boredom. He touched their imagination. Their fundamental decency was disturbed. They came out of the barn silent, not knowing what to say to each other. Even the bloody-minded sergeant thought he had gone too far, as an extremely sensual man may object to smutty stories. Dominic himself looked haggard and haunted. Before this address, whatever the attitude of his fellow-officers, he had been popular with his men. Now they watched him with misgiving.

He felt his new isolation, but he was, with less self-consciousness, like the preposterous hero of Henley's song, ready to take all the bludgeoning of chance. Yet at times he longed for human contact, if only physical.

He set off one evening for Béthune. Raife, who in spite of his preoccupation with the three F's was the only one of the company officers with universal goodwill, wanted to come with him, but Dominic put him off. He liked Raife well enough, as much as he was capable of liking anyone at this time, but Raife treated lightly those things of which Dominic now thought with grim seriousness. The three F's for him were not merely an amusing alliteration.

When he had parted from Helena his agonized sense of loss had numbed his physical desires, and this condition had remained until the first night he had spent at Catherine Street. But that interlude had been too short to disturb his condition, which his immediate departure to the front had restored. Now the prolonged and passionate indulgence of his ten days' leave had dissolved that curious static chastity. It had also destroyed his instinct of physical fidelity to Helena, which her last letter had done nothing to revive.

When something stimulated his physical desires he no longer had any reason to repress them. Authority endorsed them, equally with his violence. The men were allowed to queue up at the red lamp.

He dined alone in the restaurant where, a month or two earlier, he had dined with Hollis. Tonight he drank the whole bottle of Volnay himself, and he thought about Hollis, almost the only person of whom he could think without confusion, without that kind of jam in his brain. He wished Hollis was there with him, that they could repeat the evening of two months earlier. He thought of the visit to the prostitute, and now that authority was his conscience, he decided to visit her after dinner. His body wanted a woman, but also in some way he felt that in going to this woman he was affirming his friendship with Hollis.

He found her alone, and she received him with her cheerful hostess's manner. But he hardly treated her as another sentient human being. When he left her he also, for the time being, had lost the feeling for Hollis which had taken him there. On the way back he passed the orchard where they had walked together in innocence. It no longer meant anything to him, no more than if he passed a shop where he had once bought some apples.

The battalion returned to the line to take part in the attack. Before they left the village at dusk the officers dined early in their separate messes. In the cottage room which was A company's mess, and probably in the others, there fell a dreadful Gethsemane depression. It was almost impossible that one of the men sitting there would not be dead in a week. It was certain that one or more of them would be wounded, perhaps with some hideous affliction, blindness or amputated legs. It was easily possible that they would all be dead. It often happened in an attack.

They could hardly speak. Finch and the other soldier-servant waiting at the table emanated the same gloom.

Even Raife had nothing to say. His three F's were only a bright idea in his head. He had not yet experienced any of them, except a little fox-hunting when staying with some cousins in Ireland. Now that the first F was to become a reality, he felt the blood not racing happy and scarlet in his veins, but like lead.

Dominic alone was calm, enclosed in his dedication to violence. Now at last he was going to fulfil the purpose for which he had left his home, to achieve the greatest orgasm, that of killing his enemy. He now accepted the enemy given him by authority. "Who dies fighting hath increase." He did not know what this meant, but Julian Grenfell's beautiful senseless poem ran in his head.

When his platoon paraded in the dusk, he saw that one of his men was drunk, for which he could be shot. In spite of Dominic's new resolution of violence, the instincts of his life hitherto continued to function, and he tried to conceal the man's condition from the sergeant. When they were in the communication trench he carried his pack. All the way into the line there was a conflict between his will to save the man, and the sergeant's will to send him back to be court-martialled and shot. Dominic although he was in a kind of mystical exaltation at the approaching fight, spent his time on the way to battle in saving a life. Technically he was a commissioned officer, above the sergeant. In practice, if a temporary or territorial subaltern, one of those easily acquired, plentiful thousands with the milk on their mouths, had overridden a valuable, long-trained, regular army sergeant in a matter of this kind, he would have been in trouble with his colonel. Dominic knew this, and he showed unusual subtlety and ingenuity in helping the man outside the sergeant's observation.

The attack was planned for sunrise on an early September morning. The night before was a long vigil of depression until the rum was given out just before zero hour.

Afterwards Dominic could not remember much about all this. It was like some mad dream, from which he only awoke in the moment of losing consciousness. Harrison was white-faced and nervous, nearly unfit to command the company. Frost was correct and dutiful, and calm through absence of imagination. Raife met Dominic once or twice during the night. He grinned and said: "My bowels are like water."

Suddenly in the stillness of the dawn, the serene empty heavens rained down hell. The men climbed out of the trenches and stumbled across under the protection of the barrage. It was as on the evening of the raid. A section would be blotted out by a shell. A man would fall over like a doll. The noise produced an intense exhilaration in Dominic, as loud explosions do in Mediterranean people. In this daze of excitement he went forward, approaching the final orgasm. This only was fixed in his mind. He carried a revolver in his hand and a Mills bomb in each of his side pockets. He would kill the enemy who faced him. At last in all the row and confusion, when he hardly knew what was happening, when from his limited view the battle had no order or design, he found himself face to face with a German soldier, and he lifted his revolver to fire.

As he did so he looked in the German's eyes. He was a boy of about the age of Hollis, to whom he had an odd resemblance. In the half second while he lifted his revolver, he gave a faint glance of recognition, to which the boy made an involuntary response. But Dominic did not stay the instinctive movement of the hand, and in that instant of mutual human recognition, with eye open to eye, he shot the boy, who fell dead a yard in front of him, rolling over and over as Hollis had rolled in the dew. He stood for a moment, bewildered, and another German soldier stepped over his dead companion and plunged a bayonet into Dominic's body. His part in the orgasm had become passive.

## CHAPTER NINE

DOMINIC WAS NOT KILLED. THE BAYONET MISSED his heart and his stomach, but he lost four pints of blood to nourish those Flanders poppies which had become the symbol of the devouring jaws, making it all sound pastoral. He was sent to a hospital at the base, where his wound was given time to heal. After that he was taken to England, to another hospital for semi-convalescent officers in Hertfordshire, which turned out to be the converted house of Sylvia's friend Hermione Maine. She lived in a house in the village but was the commandant of the hospital.

Although Sylvia made use of her as a "Bunbury" she did not always tell her why, and Hermione had never heard of Dominic except vaguely as someone to whom Sylvia had been engaged before she knew her, and she had forgotten his surname. When she heard that a lieutenant called Langton was coming, the name conveyed nothing to her, and she asked: "Can he walk?" When she was told that he was very weak and had better be downstairs, she said: "Put him in Ward IV," which was her former dining-room.

This was a large room with white plaster decorations, a domed and coffered ceiling, round arches over symmetrically placed doors and twin white columns. It was on the east side of the house, and opened on io a terrace above the park. On a sunny morning it appeared cheerful enough, but in the afternoons it was cold and bleak. Its classical austerity had formerly been relieved by the warm colours of eighteenth-century portraits, rich stuffs and red faces; but when a young officer in the returning high spirits of recovery had flung a fork and lodged it in one of these faces, the portraits had been removed.

In the afternoon Dominic lay in this cold hollow, looking across to where beyond the park an autumn wood glowed in the afternoon sun. In a dim half-conscious way he was affected by the design of the room, cold and bare and traditional, the life-giving colour removed. He felt now that his life somehow corresponded with the room, that it was an empty arbitrary inheritance, from which he could see, but because of his weakness, never reach the green and golden woods where natural life throbbed in its free rhythm. He thought of the wild berries and the hazel nuts, and the plumage of pheasants. He was empty as the room, as cold and as static. There was no warmth in the atmosphere of his mind. Again the air had become thin, and the law of gravity had changed. His mind had become a traditional room which had lost its natural use and its meaning.

Yet in the room of his mind one picture remained, one from which he could never escape; whether his eyes were open or closed; whether the morning sun made the columns an echo of Greece and Rome, or whether towards evening it became a dead eighteenth-century hollow. As we are said to see all the scenes of our life at the moment of death, so he, conversely, was to see the scene of what could have been his death, for the remainder of his life. He still lived in the half-second in which he exchanged with the German boy that glance of human recognition, and at the same time shot him dead. As he lay weakly returning to life that face was before him. The stronger he became the stronger grew the image. As he went into the attack one of his ideas, a traditional picture in his mind, was that he would avenge Hollis. But he had shot Hollis in the moment of recognition. Now his mind was like the hollow room without the sun, and in it the only picture was that of the German boy, with his open friendly eyes at the moment of death.

Hermione Maine went daily round the wards. She smiled at Dominic but did not speak to him at first as he looked so weak and withdrawn. She was interested in his haggard-handsome face with its Mediterranean look of sorrow, a deep sorrow of being, rather than grief at external misfortune. One day when he seemed stronger she stopped by his bed and asked automatically: "Have you everything you want?"

"Yes, thank you," said Dominic, though he had nothing he wanted. Everything he had wanted had vanished, like the pictures from the walls.

"No one has come to see you. And the sister says that you have no letters."

"I'm an Australian. My letters are forwarded from the bank. They don't know I'm here yet."

"Oh, they must be told at once," said Hermione, with a commandant's efficiency. "I'll write myself. Which is your bank?"

He told her and she asked: "Haven't you any friends in England?"

"I have a cousin in London, but she's very old. She couldn't come here."

"Haven't you any friends?"

"I have some friends at Dilton near Frome. But they are fairly old, too. I couldn't ask them to come all this way."

"Dilton?" Hermione paused and then asked: "What is your Christian name?"

"Dominic."

"Oh, you are *that* man! How extraordinary!" she exclaimed.

"Why?"

"You were engaged to Sylvia. She is one of my greatest friends. She must come to see you. She often comes down. Have you made it up? After the broken engagement, I mean."

"Yes, we did. Her father is my colonel," said Dominic.

His face became haggard with weariness. To think of Sylvia was an effort for him. His passive look of sorrow became one of active pain. She saw that she had tired him and said: "You had better sleep now." As she went out she said to the nurse: "Mr Langton is a friend of Mrs Wesley-Maude's. See that he has everything he wants."

As a result of Hermione's writing to the bank, there arrived a few mornings later a batch of letters for him, mostly from Australia, but also two or three others, including one from Raife and one from Sylvia. He opened Raife's first. It dealt with the life closest to him and so would be the least effort to read. In the base hospital he had heard rumours of the fate of the battalion, and this letter confirmed them. Harrison came through all right. Frost had been killed. Finch had been wounded. Raife himself was wounded. He described with ribald indelicacy the nature of his wounds, and also wrote that Dominic was likely to get the Military Cross. Dominic wondered why.

Again this was due to Harrison, whose attitude to him was not hostile, but only, so he told himself, disciplinarian. He was irritated by his detached manner towards the military hierarchy, and the contrast between his efficiency in the line and his independence out of it, his unconscious

[123]

and to Harrison unjustified assurance. His feelings towards Dominic were much kinder than Dominic's towards him. He really wanted his friendship, and secretly his approval. Like Lord Dilton he felt that "there was something in" Dominic, and that the approval of this indefinable "something" was necessary to his self-respect. To show that he was not unfair towards him he secured him this decoration.

Dominic lay awhile thinking of the battalion, the dead and wounded men, and then he took up his Australian letters. He looked at the postmarks so that he could read them in the order in which they had been sent. There were three from Helena. She had recovered from the disease from the sheep, and Aunt Mildred had come up from Melbourne to help. She had also found an oldish man to take Harry's place on the farm. The baby was flourishing, and now quite articulate.

His mother's letter was in the same strain of the life at Westhill, where now it was spring, and the daffodils were blooming under the gum trees along the drive. Helena's last letter was written about two days before he was wounded. She said that she had not heard from him recently. She went on to describe in detail the life on the farm, hoping to bring it, and so herself, vividly before him. She mentioned the names of the horses, the new tank she had bought to increase the supply of water to the kitchen, and she gave an amusing picture of Aunt Mildred trying with refinement to feed the pigs.

The life seemed remote to him. He could not imagine it clearly, not in all its colour. While trying to do so, he opened Sylvia's letter. It had been written some weeks earlier and had lain with the others at the bank. She had seen his name in the casualty list and had discarded her usual discretion. She began: "My dearest Dominic," and ended, "With all my love." Reading this immediately after

Helena's letter again produced the sensation of a jam in his brain. In his weak condition it stunned him, and he fell asleep, his hand on the letter.

In his sleep the haunting vision returned. Again he was shooting a boy in the moment of recognition, but in the confusion of his dream the boy became Harry, whom Helena had dismissed. Then he changed into Finch, his wounded servant.

Hermione Maine also had a letter from Sylvia on that morning, to say that she was coming down on the following day. She went to Ward IV to tell Dominic, and found him sitting up but asleep, his head sagged on his chest, his hand on a letter. She saw that it was on the same coloured blue paper as her letter from Sylvia. She could read the only words which Dominic's hand left uncovered: "With all my love, Sylvia." She did not wake him up, but came again in the afternoon, to ask him to have tea with herself and Sylvia in her office the following afternoon.

"Have you seen her since you returned to England?" she asked quizzically.

"No, I was brought straight here," said Dominic.

"I mean since you came back from Australia."

"Yes. I saw her at Dilton and in London," he added, not wanting to be more misleading than was necessary.

"She didn't tell me," said Hermione, rather cross but amused. "How very sly of her. I shall haff her about it."

"No, don't," said Dominic, with the calm authority which either impressed or irritated those to whom it was directed. It piqued Hermione.

"Why not?"

"It would not be advisable."

She laughed shortly and left him. No one had spoken to her like that since she left the schoolroom, certainly not in her own house. She really ought to snub him, but she did not see how she could snub someone who not only looked like an El Greco *pietà*, but whose weakness clothed him with indifference, and who also seemed to contain an extreme humility within an implacable pride. She thought Sylvia had been a fool to give him up for Wesley-Maude.

Dominic now spent two or three hours every day out of bed, either on the terrace if it was fine, or sitting up in a chair in the ward. His greatest effort so far was to walk up the main staircase to Hermione's "office" on the first floor. This was really her own sitting-room, left unchanged when the house was turned into a hospital. The furniture was not unlike that of Sylvia's toy palatial drawing-room. There were similar kingwood and ormolu commodes, French chairs, and a grandiose looking-glass over the Adam mantelpiece. When Dominic, a little breathless from climbing the stairs, came into this room, and saw Sylvia sitting there alone – Hermione perhaps intentionally was attending to some duty – it was almost a reconstruction of when he had been shown into her drawing-room at Catherine Street. She was wearing the same kind of clothes as on that morning when he met her in Green Park, a dark fur-collared coat, the pearls, a black velvet hat on her golden hair.

In her eyes as she looked up at him, was an almost anxious, questioning look. This look and the echo of Catherine Street seemed to make a demand on him which he could not meet. He did not know whether the demand was an impossible one on his weak body, or if it was on something else, on his mind that it should in some way conform to and accept the limits of her own.

When they shook hands his was lifeless. Although they were alone he did not attempt to kiss her, and she saw no memory of their love in his eyes. She drew up a chair for him to the tea-table, and she said in her ordinary, rather cold conventional voice: "How are you? Was it too much for you to walk upstairs?"

"No. I'm getting better. But I have to go slowly."

They talked a little stiffly about his health, and then Hermione came in, and Sylvia found it more easy to talk to him.

"Why didn't you let me know you were here?" she asked him.

"I haven't written to anybody yet."

"He wasn't strong enough," said Hermione.

"If you're strong enough to walk upstairs you can write a letter."

"No. It's much harder to write a letter," said Dominic. They laughed and the atmosphere was easier.

"Does father know where you are?" asked Sylvia. "He'll be very hurt if you don't write to him."

Sylvia was talking with the language used between intimates, critical but friendly. Hermione noticed that Dominic's response was not on the same level.

"I shall write to him," he said, "in a little while." He seemed more to be deciding something for himself than to be speaking to Sylvia.

Hermione poured out the tea and the conversation became general. She was puzzled by them. Dominic seemed more remote than ever, not stimulated and enlivened, as she had hoped he would be, by Sylvia's presence. And she could see that Sylvia, beneath her rather hard social manner, was not happy. Sylvia had once helped her out of a fairly innocent scrape when she was engaged, and in gratitude she was willing to be useful to her when possible. She was a little uneasy at being asked to pretend that she was staying with her, but Sylvia gave the excuse that her mother was always pestering her to go down to Dilton. She did not approve of Sylvia having an "affair" with Dominic, especially while Maurice was at the front, but she thought that it would be mildly amusing to confront her with her former lover, and might also help to revitalize Dominic. When she saw "With all my love" on his letter from Sylvia, she had already invited her.

But Dominic, holding his teacup, looked more than ever like an El Greco *pietà*. It would certainly be safe to leave them alone together, and with a sort of muddled good-nature towards Sylvia, she made the excuse of seeing another patient, and left the room. When she came back they were sitting as she had left them, and apparently in silence. He looked so exhausted that Hermione said: "I think you had better go back to bed."

"Shall I help you downstairs?" asked Sylvia.

"I can manage," said Dominic. "I'll hold on to the banister."

They shook hands again. He felt utterly weak and inadequate, unable to meet the demand of her mere presence. He tried to smile, but the effort was pitiful. He thought that he must say something and the only words that came were: "It was good of you to come down."

Hermione went with him to the stairs, and then fearing that he might fall, took his arm and guided him down. When she came back to her sitting-room, she found to her astonishment that Sylvia was crying.

Dominic took off his clothes – it was the first time that he had been completely dressed – and climbed into his iron bed. In the dead traditional room the other weak and wounded men lay in their black beds, either asleep or reading by shaded lamps. The wood beyond the park was veiled in blue mist, and further obscured by the reflections on the glass. Everything was still and fading, the autumnal wood, the bleak room where there was no colour left on the walls, as across the park the glowing leaves had fallen from the trees. Upstairs in Hermione's room the colour remained, the tradition still lived, but it was no longer alive for him. Even Sylvia, so much herself in that kind of room, because of it, became unreal to him. She had been a symbol of the things he had missed, but which now were dead. He could not feel any contact with her.

Between her face and his was the face of the boy he had shot. Because of the response in that boy's eyes as he shot him, he could no longer meet her eyes. This had become not so much an emotional obsession, as a reasoned perception of his mind. He reasoned about everything connected with that incident.

He was better here, he thought, in the dead room, under the bare walls, the cold pillars and the hollow dome, than in the room above where the old life remained. He could not respond to the rays of its colour. There had never been tenderness between himself and Sylvia, only the passion of their bodies. Now he saw clearly, with his mind but not with his heart, that she had tenderness to offer him. He was puzzled, but he could find no response to it.

In a few days he had a letter from Lord Dilton, who wrote:

*I was very sorry to hear that you were so badly wounded, but Sylvia tells me that you are now well on the way to recovery. I wrote to you in France when I saw your name in the casualty list, but things were a bit chaotic at the time and I suppose you did not get the letter. The first battalion was badly cut up.*

*If you have nowhere to go when you leave the hospital, Edith and I would be very pleased if you came here. It would not be exciting, but we should do our best to make you comfortable. If you don't help me to drink it, some of the best wine will go over. We shall put you on the establishment when you're fit again, which I hope will be soon. You've done well, but I am glad that you're out of it.*

He did not reply to this letter until he had left Hermione's hospital, a few weeks later.

## CHAPTER TEN

WHEN HE LEFT THE HOSPITAL DOMINIC WENT TO the little hotel in Mayfair where he was now known. On arrival he rang up Cousin Emma's house. She was out, but he said that he would come round to collect some luggage he had left there. The parlourmaid told him that it was not ready to take away. The suitcases were in the boxroom, and his clothes had been put away with camphor in chests of drawers. They would need to be aired and pressed. He said that did not matter, and he took a taxi down to Brompton Square. The parlourmaid helped him pack his clothes. When they had done this she asked him to wait to see Cousin Emma who would be back soon, and sorry to miss him, but he did not feel sufficiently braced to meet her, and he only left a grateful message.

He went back to the hotel and changed into a creased and smelly grey suit. Then he went out and sat in the park near Stanhope Gate. He wore no overcoat as he hoped that the fresh air would take the smell of camphor from his suit. But he was soon cold and he went back and lit the gas fire in his hotel bedroom. He hung his coat on a chair before the fire and lay down on the bed, and tried to think what to do.

This hotel room was now the only room he had, apart from his farm, where his wife and child lived on the other side of the world. But his farm had almost ceased to have material reality for him, in spite of Helena's evocative letters. It had been too long an unattainable dream, and the letters had the nature of a medieval description of heaven. He had as so often in his life followed his impulse without seeing the next step. He had put on civilian clothes, and then saw no direction in which he could turn. He had left the hollow room, the dead tradition in which he had lived hitherto, but he had no other dwelling, no one even that he could go to see. Cousin Emma would be incredulous and hostile when she saw him no longer in his smart uniform. When he thought of going to see Sylvia the jam at once came violently down in his brain. He could not even give himself a reason why he could not see her.

He could not go to see Colonel Rodgers, even if he were in London, though now that he had been wounded and could, if he wished, put the ribbon of the Military Cross on his tunic, if he were wearing it, there was no one who would welcome him more warmly. He had something to establish himself with, to make him respected among his fellows, and he could not use it. To do so would be to ignore all that had happened in these last months, to ignore the boy whom he had shot, and to whom in some curious fashion he now felt his life belonged. With that feeling the jam in his brain was eased. He found that at last he could write to Lord Dilton. He crossed the room and sat down at a table where there was some stamped hotel paper in a box. He wrote:

*Dear Colonel,*
*You have always been such a good friend to me that it is hard to write what I must say now. I am not*

*coming back to the battalion. I have taken off my uniform and shall not wear it again. I cannot give my clear reasons in a letter, but I know that I must do this. I cannot do anything else. If there was any possible way in which I could avoid giving this return for your help and kindness, I would do it. I realise that you will have to take some disciplinary action against me. I shall be waiting at this hotel.*

*Yours sincerely,*
*Dominic Langton*

He went downstairs, bought a stamp at the reception desk, and himself took out the letter to post it. He had to be absolutely certain that it would go. He was more peaceful when he returned to his room, knowing that the letter was irrevocably in the pillar box. He had a light dinner sent up to him and went to bed, where he slept until eleven o'clock the next morning.

There was a telegram on his breakfast tray: "Meet me at B——'s Club one o'clock tomorrow. Dilton."

Dominic spent the rest of the day drowsily in his room, except for a short walk in the park. The journey to London and the unaccustomed activity of the previous day had used up his slight reserves of strength. But the next morning, after another long sleep, he felt reasonably well again.

He dressed himself as tidily as possible. His civilian shirts were quite fresh, and unlike his suits, smelled faintly of lavender. The gas fire had drawn most of the smell of camphor from his coat, but not all the creases. His hat was Australian, with a rather wide brim. As he walked down St James's Street, where all the young men were in uniform, he looked rather as if he had been dressed in a waxworks.

Lord Dilton was waiting for him in the hall at B——'s. He gave a slight start when he saw Dominic in civilian clothes. Although he had read in his letter that he would be wearing them, he had been so disturbed by his statement that he would not be returning to the battalion that he had not taken in the rest. He shook hands in a serious friendly way and said: "I'm glad you could get here. Are you quite fit now?"

"Yes," said Dominic. "I'm much better, thank you, sir."

"Well, we'd better go and find some luncheon."

Lord Dilton, forgetting that Dominic would not be in uniform, had intended to give him lunch at his club, but his appearance was a little odd. In his wax-works style clothes he did not look like an officer in mufti. He thought Dominic must be suffering from slight shell-shock, and hoped to persuade him to have further treatment and then return to the depot. He wanted to have as little attention as possible drawn to his present aberration. If he succeeded he did not want to be asked why Dominic had dressed like that to lunch with his colonel. He took him along to the grill room of the Carlton Hotel. When they were seated he said: "We'll have something to eat first, and then talk things over."

During luncheon he talked about his herd of black cattle, and other things to do with farming. When they had their coffee, he said: "Perhaps we had better go back and find some quiet room at the club where we can talk."

Dominic demurred. He did not want to talk as Lord Dilton's guest, above all in a place like B——'s, where the tradition, which (in the bleak dining-room ward) he had felt to be dead, was alive and where every influence around them would be against him. He suggested that they should go back to his hotel. Lord Dilton thought it wise to humour him. In fact he preferred this himself, and they took a taxi there.

There was a small public room at the back of the hotel,

furnished with a mahogany table, two leather armchairs, a statuette of Cupid and Psyche, a copy of *Who's Who* and a telephone directory. Dominic had never seen this room in use, so they went there, and sat in the leather armchairs on either side of a gas fire.

"You wrote to me," said Lord Dilton, "that you couldn't give me the reasons for your attitude in a letter. Can you give them now?"

"I'll try," said Dominic, but he began again to feel the stoppage in his brain, and he sat back in his chair without speaking. After a while Lord Dilton said: "You know the seriousness of the position you want to take, and its consequences for others besides yourself?"

Dominic had not thought of the consequences for others, except perhaps Helena, and in his mind she was too far away to be much affected. But the mention of these consequences made the jam in his brain worse. He felt as if he were an ant trying to oppose the downhill progress of a steam roller. He closed his eyes trying to think how to begin.

Lord Dilton felt some responsibility for his attitude, which, apart from the friendship he had for him and the fact that their families were old territorial neighbours with links through marriage, was one of the reasons why he had come to see him. From any other subaltern he would have thought a letter like Dominic's crazy insolence, and would have put the proper machinery in motion to bring him to his senses. But Dominic had succeeded to this extent in life, that he had brought people to expect and even to accept his unpredictable behaviour.

Lord Dilton after his conversation at dinner on that night during Dominic's leave, when he was returning from Cornwall, had twinges of conscience. He thought that a colonel had no right to talk in that way about the war to one of his subalterns who was on active service, even if he was a friend outside the army. He was a responsible and conventional country gentleman, but the conventions to which he subscribed were being superseded. He believed strongly in authority, but also that authority should be patriarchal and benevolent; whereas now, directed by the press magnates and political adventurers, it was becoming rapacious and destructive of what he regarded as civilization. As with Dominic, his conventions no longer fitted the circumstances, so that, although very different from him, he had in a lesser degree the same inner conflict. He thought that he might be responsible for planting seeds in the hotbed of Dominic's mind, which in the cool English earth of his own, did not produce such reckless and disproportionate growths.

"What consequences do you mean?" asked Dominic at last.

"If you refuse to fight you will bring disgrace on your wife and child; also it will be a black mark against your regiment."

"I'm sorry, sir," said Dominic. "But whatever I do harms someone. That would be a lesser injury. At least I don't take their lives."

Lord Dilton was going to say: "There are worse things than losing your life," but although he believed that on rare occasions this was true, he felt suddenly nauseated at the idea of using the jargon that induced the country to fling a whole generation into the Moloch jaws.

"If you feel that way," he said, "you can come back to the depot, and we'll put you on the establishment for the rest of the war. You've done your share. You've been decorated and badly wounded. No one could criticise you. You've done very well."

"I don't feel that I've done well and I couldn't go on teaching others to do what I won't do myself."

Lord Dilton was surprised to find that he was relieved at this refusal, but he said: "It's right to fight for your country."

"But I wasn't fighting for my country. I would do that to defend Waterpark and Dilton. They are all of this country that I know. But you said on that night when I dined with you that we were fighting to ruin ourselves, to wipe out the Diltons and the Waterparks."

Lord Dilton looked gloomily at the gas fire. "I was afraid that was it," he said. "I should not have spoken to you like that. I was feeling sore about Wolverhampton, who was an old friend of mine."

"But what you said was true, sir."

"We can't take the law into our own hands. If everyone did what he thought right we'd have anarchy. A government must function, even a bad one, which I admit we have – damned bad one. Anyhow the government does allow for these conscientious objectors."

He used the words reluctantly, unwilling to believe that they could apply to a personal friend and an officer in his regiment.

"But I'm not a conscientious objector," said Dominic. "I would fight for Waterpark and for my farm in Australia if anyone threatened them. But they are not threatened, except by our own government. That's what you said. When conscripts fight conscripts they are not defending anything. Neither is a menace to the other, or they would not be conscripted. The murder is forced on them from behind, by their governments."

"There must be a government," repeated Lord Dilton, "and I suppose, newspapers."

"The government has no Divine Right. It's only a Tweedledum agreeing to have a battle with a German Tweedledee. They could stop tomorrow if they wanted to.

If anyone attacks me or what belongs to me, I'll fight; but I won't commit murder because someone else tells me to. That's what I'm really trying to say."

That was the nearest he could get to the true cause of his attitude, the one particular murder which he could not bring himself to mention. He advanced arguments about the politicians and about the Wolverhamptons, because he thought that they would be acceptable to Lord Dilton. He believed that they were true, as much as he knew about them, but they were not his concern. What made it impossible for him to fight again was the brief exchange of human recognition as he shot the German boy.

He believed that then he had violated every good thing he knew, all his passion for the beauty of the created world, which he had felt when he watched the Spanish divers, when he had held the chestnut bud in his hand on the steps of the village church. More, that glance came from the recognition of their deepest selves, a recognition of kind, which wiped out all the material obligation of their opposed circumstances.

In that act he had violated the two things to which his whole being responded in worship; the beauty of a living human body, all the miracle of its movement and thought; and the relation of two souls in brotherhood. He had affronted both nature and God, which cannot be separated. Although it was his own single act that overwhelmed him, he was also oppressed by his awareness of the accumulated anguish of the war, the senseless death and hideous wounds multiplied and multiplied and multiplied.

He went on advancing arguments which he thought would appeal to Lord Dilton, about the responsibility of governments and the fate of the landed gentry; but they were a deathly weariness to him. He was only filled with a passion of repudiation, which his mind was too ill-informed to present logically, and his body too weak to support.

"But it's anarchy," Lord Dilton protested. "You can't expect me to support you."

"I don't expect you to, sir," said Dominic. "But I don't believe it's anarchy. It's the real law against artificial law."

"What d'you mean by the real law?"

Dominic was silent. It was something he felt more than thought about.

"The real law is natural," he said at last.

"Nature is savage enough – red in tooth and claw."

"It's natural to kill your real enemies, those who threaten you; or to kill animals you want to eat. It's not natural to kill people you don't know, because you and they are told by Lloyd George and Bethmann-Hollweg, or whoever it is, to kill each other. Lloyd George and Bethmann-Hollweg are not greater than God, to vet his laws, but we behave as if they were. I found that out in the very moment that I was wounded. Not because I was wounded, but just before, and I will never commit murder again. Nothing shall make me, nothing at all. I am sorry, sir."

Lord Dilton sat back in his chair. Dominic had spoken with such absolute conviction that he saw it was useless to continue the argument. In fact Dominic looked completely exhausted. The abandoned posture of his body showed that he had nothing more to say.

"Can you wait a bit before doing anything definite?" asked Lord Dilton. "It's obvious that you're not fit yet."

"What I feel has nothing to do with being C.3.," said Dominic. "I only know that I mustn't serve any longer."

'Who tells you that you mustn't?'

Dominic puckered his forehead. "The Holy Ghost, I suppose," he replied.

"You are not serious!" said Lord Dilton angrily.

"It's the only way I can explain it," said Dominic.

They sat silent for a few minutes. Lord Dilton looked

flushed and bothered. At last he appeared to come to a decision.

"Until you're fit, there's no need to declare yourself," he said.

"Everyone will know. They'll ask why I'm not wearing uniform."

"You're wounded and on leave. Tell 'em to go to the devil," said Lord Dilton, who was himself in mufti. "When I was young, soldiers didn't go about in private houses wearing uniform. But I suppose it pleases these young fellows they have now. Anyhow, will you do nothing for a bit?"

"Nothing is about all I can do," said Dominic, smiling bleakly. The old friendship between them grew stronger.

"Will you come down to Dilton until you're quite fit? We won't talk about it until then. Put it in cold storage for a while."

"Wouldn't I be in a false position there?"

"Of course not. It's my house," said Lord Dilton curtly.

"I mean Lady Dilton might not like my being there if she knew."

"She won't know, nor will anyone else. You haven't spoken of this till now?"

"No, sir. I had to tell you first."

"Good. Will you come down tonight, or would you rather wait till tomorrow?"

Dominic said that he would rather wait. He went with Lord Dilton to the door of the hotel, where he thanked him for not being angry.

"As a matter of fact, I was damned annoyed," said Lord Dilton, but he laughed.

Dominic went up and lay on his bed. Having made this arrangement with Lord Dilton, there was now, he thought, no reason why he should not go to see Sylvia. But he could not feel that there was any relationship between them. He had not felt any when they met in Hermione Maine's sitting-room. All their passionate unions, their abandonment in that moonlit bedroom in Penzance, were like something he had once read in a book. Not a single fibre of his body vibrated at the memory. With his persistent habit of expecting other people's feelings to correspond with his own, in spite of repeated shocks from the discovery that they did not, he imagined that she too had passed through a similar change of emotional climate. If she came down to Dilton while he was there, he thought that it would be mildly pleasant.

But she did not go down while he was there, partly because she did not want to repeat the humiliation of their meeting at Hermione's, which she thought would be certain when she heard that Dominic had been in London without letting her know. Another reason for her not coming was the extreme caution she observed, and she was afraid that if her mother saw them together, she might instinctively divine, from some expression when their eyes met, even if it was not one of love, what had passed between them.

Dominic went down by the afternoon train, and in the evening he dined alone with the Diltons. There was the same peaceful domestic atmosphere as on the night nearly two years ago when he had arrived unexpectedly from Australia, and it gave him a sense of homecoming. His problems seemed less urgent, and to belong to some other region.

Soon after dinner Lady Dilton said that Dominic should go to bed, and her husband left for the depot. In the hall he told Dominic to take things easily, to do what he liked, and to put his difficulties out of his mind for the present. He had to build himself up.

"I can't come over every evening," he said, "as I have to dine in mess. I hope you'll find some way of amusing yourself. You can browse in the library, and when you feel like it you can go out and shoot a pheasant."

Dominic slept deeply through the silent night. At the hospital there had been the slight noises made by other patients in the ward, the screens, the bedpans, and the feeling of an institution; in London there was the traffic. Here there was absolute stillness, until at eight o'clock the housemaid came in quietly and drew back the curtains, revealing a soft grey morning with a rain that was little more than a mist. He felt that if the housemaid stopped her quiet movements, he would hear the mist falling on the grass in the park. His breakfast, with porridge and cream, with eggs laid last evening, and all the home-grown produce, butter and honey, that kept the Diltons' cheeks so rosy, was brought up to his room. The tray was sparkling with soft Georgian silver. He supposed that the linen was clean at the hospital, but it did not seem to have had the virginal whiteness of his tray cloth. The pillow was softer, the sheets were slippery-smooth. The fire which the housemaid had just lighted was crackling up the chimney, and the flames were reflected in the chintz, covered with sprawling roses, of the curtains and the chairs. The material conditions were those of absolute security and peace, and they affected his state of mind.

Lady Dilton came up to see him after breakfast and asked the usual questions: "How did you sleep?" "Have you everything you want?" So tough and bossy were those in good health, with an invalid, especially with a wounded soldier; she was all solicitude, and would almost retard his recovery with excessive cosseting. She told him not to get up until he felt inclined as it was a damp morning.

"If you do get up," she said, "you can come and help me with my envelopes." Her envelopes, like the temperature of

[141]

the bath water, had become one of the *leit-motifs* of life at Dilton during the war.

At eleven o'clock he dressed and went down to Lady Dilton's sitting-room. She immediately rang the bell and ordered a glass of hot milk for him. When he had drunk it they settled on either side of the writing table and addressed envelopes. The retriever lay on the hearthrug with his head in the fender.

"Byng," she said crossly, "don't lie like that. You'll roast your brains." The dog rose lazily and came over and put his head on her knee. She took no notice of him and he went back and flopped against the fender. The peaceful routine of the day went on.

In the afternoon Colonel Rodgers came over to see Dominic. Since early in the war the hour of tea at Dilton had been advanced to half past four. One of the colonel's articles of faith was that "no gentleman has his tea before five o'clock". He could not bear to think that his own sister tarnished her coronet by this common and unclean habit, and he always arrived at five, when the tea was stewed and tepid, so that his visits began with peevish recriminations. He had been told by Lord Dilton that he was not to ask Dominic questions about the war, as it was doctor's orders; but his annoyance at being given a cup of pale lukewarm liquid tasting faintly of tar, made him ignore this injunction. He asked at once: "Why aren't you in uniform?"

Dominic flushed, but Lady Dilton said brusquely: "Because he's more comfortable like that."

"You must have your photograph taken in uniform with your M.C. up," said Colonel Rodgers.

He obeyed his brother-in-law's instructions to the extent of not actually asking for the description of a battle, but he talked only of matters connected with the war, and the prospects of smashing the Germans in the spring.

Lord Dilton's attitude towards Dominic was not only one of sympathy with a point of view which he believed was largely justified. It was part of a plan. He hoped that Dominic, receiving kindness and friendship in the familiar places of his youth, would be brought to conform to the pattern of life there, and abandoning his self-ostracism would agree to return to the depot for the rest of the war.

His wife told him that Marcus had come over to tea, half an hour late as usual, that he had talked about nothing but the war, and that as soon as he left Dominic had gone to bed with a violent headache. Lord Dilton, exaggerating what he believed to be true, had told her that he was suffering from a form of shell-shock.

He was very angry when he heard this. He was kind, just, and often easy-going, but he was also an autocrat. He had been the most important person in his neighbourhood since he was a young man, and he regarded any form of disobedience as a personal affront. Dominic's letter at first had made him more than "damned annoyed" but his anger had cooled quickly, partly because Dominic had done well at the front, but more because of a special feeling he had had for him since he first became aware of him in his seventeenth year, which he could only explain as he did then by saying: "There's something in that boy." He rang up Colonel Rodgers and "gave him hell", forbidding him to come to Dilton again while Dominic was there.

This was a boon to Dominic. He realized how reluctant he had been to see the colonel. When they had lived at Waterpark, with Colonel Rodgers in the dower-house across the meadow, he had always been in his company. He had fastened on him as a disciple in his cult of death and violence. The colonel had stimulated in him that black inherited streak, which had come into his conscious mind in the nightmare in the French train. He had an old affection for him, but the source of its nourishment was deathly.

. There was a succession of days of drizzle. Except for a walk in the park, when Dominic was not helping Lady Dilton with her envelopes, or driving with her to deliver them, he spent most of his time in the library. He was not educated in the ordinary sense of the word. After his failure at school he had only technical training, either in agriculture or in the army. But he had been brought up in an educated atmosphere, though a dilettante one. He had travelled and had been accustomed all his life to hear a kind of philosophical conversation, the speculations of people with curious minds, who also sought their pleasure mostly in unselfconscious aesthetic appreciation. He knew the names of the great creative artists in every field, and had a dim idea of the nature of their achievements, but no exact knowledge of any of them. This contributed to his sense of being outside the pale of ordinary people, though those from whom he felt most excluded, his immediate relatives, were not in his sense ordinary. They did not fit any pattern except that of their own group.

He thought that with this library and his leisure he might begin to dispel his ignorance. He took down a translation of the *Dialogues of Plato*, and found to his surprise that they were easy to read. When Lord Dilton next came over to dine he talked of them eagerly. A new planet had swept into his ken. Lord Dilton was pleased. His plan for Dominic seemed to be working out. Nothing could be better than that he should build himself up in the ordered life of this household, and fill his mind with ideas remote from immediate problems. He advised Dominic to broaden his outlook by reading the literature of other times and countries. This had an unfortunate result – unfortunate for his plan.

Dominic searched along the shelves for translations of the literature of other countries. One of his dim cultural ideas was that the height of European civilization was reached in French literature of the sixteenth to the eighteenth centuries. He took down the Duc de Sully's book on war, and read of how the princes of that time made war, ravishing cities and slaughtering the people, with no excuse beyond their own vanity, greed and ambition. It seemed to him to apply exactly to the situation in Europe at the moment. He was excited, and could hardly wait for Lord Dilton to come to dine the next evening to show him his discovery. He was convinced now that his attitude was supported by the best authority. On the same morning, glancing into a book, he had read: "The good man tries to prevent others experiencing his own sufferings; the evil man finds compensation in seeing them repeated in others."

The next evening when he had shut the dining-room door behind Lady Dilton, he returned to the table, and taking Sully's book from the pocket of his dinner jacket, he showed the most forceful passage to Lord Dilton, who read it, and then said: "Yes. You see human nature does not change."

"But it's not human nature, sir," replied Dominic, "the people didn't want their cities sacked then, any more than the conscripts want to be butchered today. It's only a few men at the top of each country who want it, to fill their own pockets or satisfy their personal ambitions. You told me that at this very table."

Their conversation became more or less a repetition of that in the back room of the Mayfair hotel. Lord Dilton looked bothered and a little impatient.

"We can't go over it all again," he said. "Even if we agreed, we are not in a position to do anything about it." He rose from the table and they went into the sitting-room.

Lord Dilton saw that his plan for Dominic was not working out. He could not stay on indefinitely at Dilton. As soon as he was quite fit, which would not be long now, he would either have to rejoin his unit or be arrested. When he left for the depot he said: "I wouldn't stay indoors reading when it's fine. Why don't you go out with a gun?"

Dominic wanted to please him in any way he could. On the following afternoon he took the gun he had been lent, called Byng, the retriever, and walked down a field of stubble near a wood to the west of the house. When he was about fifty yards from the wood, a pheasant rose clear on his left. Dominic fired. The pheasant fell in the stubble and the dog retrieved it.

This was the first shot he had fired since he had killed the German boy. Though then it was from a revolver and now from an ordinary double-barrelled gun, the report was much the same. It was enough to bring back that scene in a flash of memory. The response to his recognition, the split second of surprise as the bullet went through his heart, and then the body rolling over and over, as Hollis had rolled in the dew. He had killed the German boy and now he had killed this bird. In some crazy way they were identified in his mind. He stood in a kind of dazed horror, touched with the same self-disgust as when he had awakened from his nightmare in the train. He barely restrained an impulse to fling away the finely made gun. He did not take the dead bird from the dog and put it in his game bag, but turned back towards the house, the dog following him, proud and contented to be carrying the bird.

Lord Dilton was concerned about Dominic, and in the evening he came over again to dine at home. He was pleased when he heard that he had been out shooting, but worried again at his withdrawn manner, and his silence at dinner. When Edith had left the room he asked him if he were not well.

"I'm well in body," said Dominic, "but I don't feel well in my mind."

"Can't you cure that yourself?" asked Lord Dilton. "Especially if you're aware of it. Don't think of things that disturb you. Think as much as you can of normal things, the ordinary activities of life."

"The ordinary activities of life make me think of other things," said Dominic. "If I read I come across things that disturb my mind; or if I go out shooting. I can't go out shooting any more. I don't think it's wrong. We have to eat. But it does something to me." He put his hand against his forehead. "There is something in my mind which normally I don't know is there. Then I do some ordinary thing, reading or shooting, and suddenly I get a kind of jam in my brain. I can't let my thoughts turn in any direction. Then the thing in my mind reveals itself. It's as if it shows me someone who is really myself, not the self I think I am. Then I have to act as that other self wants. I must. I can't help it, and I can't explain it. I couldn't when you asked me about it in London, so I said 'the Holy Ghost', but that is what I meant. Sometimes we say things that are true before we know what we are saying. The truth follows our words. I suppose it sounds mad."

Lord Dilton looked at him gravely and attentively. He saw that there was little hope of bringing him back to lead the life of an army officer. He did not think that Dominic was mad, but he thought that he really was suffering from shell-shock, that it was not merely a convenient fiction to say so. Though he was sorry that he could not restore him to conventional behaviour, in one way he was relieved, as it justified further medical treatment and would avoid scandal.

"What you say is outside my experience," he said, "so I can't judge it. It is more the subject for a doctor."

"Perhaps there was so much violence in my blood," said Dominic, "that it has fused itself and there is none left."

"It may be so," said Lord Dilton, but as if humouring him. He pushed back his chair, and putting his hand behind the candle flames, he blew them out.

In his wife's sitting-room he suggested a rubber of three-handed bridge, though neither of the other two were good players. The evening was subdued, and when Edith made mistakes he did not attack her with his usual good-humoured chaff, but was quietly irritable.

When he left, Dominic as usual went out with him to his car.

"I don't think I should stay here much longer, sir," he said.

"We'll have to think what to do," Lord Dilton replied. He stood a moment in thought. Then he said, half-smiling: "You always were rather a difficult young man, Dominic."

Dominic went back to say goodnight to Lady Dilton, who was putting the cards away, puffing up the cushions, and throwing the contents of the ashtrays into the fire, things normally left to the servants, which she now did as part of her war effort.

He went despondently upstairs. The grand house seemed inimical to him, even in this peaceful room, with its rosy chintzes gleaming in the firelight, the slippery-smooth sheets turned back invitingly, the copper can of hot water covered with towels, the glass of hot milk which owing to some magic signal was always there when he came up to bed. These things for which he had been so immensely grateful when he first arrived, now seemed to belong to a life which he had already left. The hollow room in the hospital, the arches and columns of a dead tradition were more his proper dwelling place, than this house which was not yet stripped of its life and colour. Lord Dilton had said: "We must think what to do," and it was clear that the atmosphere had changed. He no longer had the feeling that they were in this together. His sympathy was withheld if not his friendship. It was his sympathy which had enabled Dominic to stay here, feeling that the tradition was still alive. But it had only been a palliative, deadening a pain, not removing its cause.

On the next day Lord Dilton went up to London, made certain enquiries, and pulled some of those strings which were so easily accessible to him. He was not used to failing in what he undertook, and it was a disagreeable experience. He was annoyed with Dominic for not making more apparent effort to control his reactions, though he now believed they were due to shell-shock. He was still intent on avoiding any public scandal, both for the sake of the regiment and of Dominic, and also from friendship for the latter's father, who was not here to help him, and whose name, long known in the county, he did not want to see blazoned across some squalid paper describing the court martial.

As his activities were mostly in the neighbourhood of Whitehall, he went along to see Sylvia. He found her sitting alone, white-faced and listless, and looking far from well. He thought that she must have bad news of Maurice, but she said: "It's only the war. Will it never stop?" This surprised him, as he had thought, though he did not put it in these words, that she was enjoying the war, with endless theatres and parties and all the excitements of political rumour. He suggested that she should come down to Dilton for a few weks and feed herself up, though there was still the continuous flow of cream, butter, game and fresh eggs from Dilton to Catherine Street.

"Dominic is there," he said. "You can cheer him up. He's probably going in a day or two."

"How is he?" she said.

"He's fit enough. But there's something the matter with his mind."

"D'you mean he's mad?" she asked horrified.

"Good God, no! I mean that he has something on his mind. It's shell-shock. I'm trying to get him into a place where they'll treat him. It's a healthy place down in Cornwall, near Penzance."

"In Cornwall!" she exclaimed. "But you can't send him there."

"Why not?" demanded her father, mystified and cross.

Sylvia tried to laugh. "I only thought it was so far away. He'll have no one to look after him."

"Dammit," said Lord Dilton, "he'll have half a dozen nurses."

"Yes, of course." They talked of other things and she gave him a whisky before he went off to Paddington. She said that she would come down in a few days, but she did not intend to go until Dominic had left.

The place in Cornwall where Lord Dilton was arranging to send Dominic was for young officers suffering from shell-shock. Some of the cases were hopeless, and it was more of a mental hospital than Lord Dilton realized. He hoped that Dominic would agree to go there and he was prepared to use a fair amount of sentimental blackmail about his family and the regiment to persuade him. He thought it possible that he might insist on a court martial to draw attention to the futility of the endless slaughter maintained merely "to keep alive the spirit of the offensive". Dominic perhaps overestimated the effect of such a protest, but it might easily be awkward for the authorities if an officer with a good record and a decoration refused to fight any longer on the grounds of chivalry and morality. It would not be good propaganda. Dominic would receive additional publicity from his associations, and from the fact that he was heir to an ancient name. The gossip-writers would probably rake up his engagement to Sylvia, and his long stay at Dilton. Her photograph might be on the front page of some rag. It would be damnably unfair to Maurice.

Lord Dilton, his blood-stream so well nourished from his farms, and inflammable with good wine, sitting alone in his first-class carriage, had a sudden access of anger. It was not directed towards Dominic but towards the newspapers. To find Sylvia looking ill and jaded by the war had further upset him. If it continued he did not see how they could escape the fate of the Wolverhamptons. So far his two sons were alive. Dick had been wounded but was back at the front. His elder son was on the brigadier-general's staff, near the front line. Either or both of them might be killed any day. They could not last indefinitely under these conditions. If his boys had to be killed for their country he could say nothing; he must accept it. But he did not believe it was for their country. The war was continuing to destroy their country. It should stop at once, by agreement, before the European social structure was wrecked beyond repair. He admitted to himself that Dominic was fundamentally right, and his anger increased.

Why not let the boy go through with it? Why not support him? Why not mobilize the few peers who had kept their heads, and saw the ruin we were racing for? They would say he was trying to save his sons. Why the devil shouldn't he try to save his sons? Damn the Welsh Baptist! Damn the press-magnates! Not one of those who were hounding the nation to ruin was an Englishman, at any rate not of the kind whom Lord Dilton thought were fitted to rule the country. Weren't there enough decent Englishmen to stop a generation being butchered to satisfy the ambitions of these adventurers? He felt the veins swelling in his forehead. He felt that he would burst with his rage. He was in uniform and if anyone else had been in the carriage, they would have imagined that this apoplectic colonel was itching to seize the Kaiser by the throat.

Before the train reached Frome he had calmed down, and his usual habit of mind reasserted itself. The structure of the government had to be supported, and Dominic could have no effect. If every young man behaved like him there would be anarchy. Lord Dilton was unaware that if Dominic had come from different origins, he would not have tolerated his attitude for a moment. It was because he regarded him as a member of his own, the landed ruling class, that he accepted his protest as an expression of responsibility.

But he had misjudged the intention of Dominic, who had no wish to make a demonstration as a public martyr. He was only ready to accept the role if it was forced upon him. He was little concerned with what lay beyond his personal contacts. His present attitude was entirely the result of these; chiefly his contact with Hollis, and above all of that with the German boy. His concern was not to commit, not to train others to commit a similar murder. He did not believe that Hollis and the German boy were a menace to each other. They were forced into their artificial hostility from above. He would not help the process. That was as far as his conscience and his reason had taken him.

Lord Dilton was relieved when he told Dominic that he had arranged for him to go to the hospital in Cornwall, that he did not have to use any sentimental blackmail. Dominic was even pleased when he heard that there would be a doctor who dealt with mental difficulties, who could help him to relieve the jam in his brain.

Before he left Dilton, a few days later, he borrowed the bicycle which he had used on the day after his arrival from Australia, and rode once more over to Waterpark. He wanted to look again at the place which one day presumably would be his. He was curious about his own attitude towards it. He wanted to know how much he still felt it to be his home. He rode through the white gate, with its notice, "Wheels to Waterpark House only", and up the short avenue to the door in the crumbling garden wall – the old, inconvenient but unchanged way of reaching the front door. A new parlourmaid answered the bell. He gave his name and asked if he might see Mr Cecil.

He was shown into the drawing-room and in a few moments Mr Cecil appeared. Although rather more amiable than on Dominic's first visit, he still complained about the repairs needed, and he pointed out the patch of damp which had appeared again on the staircase wall. Altogether the house looked a little bleak. It had a negative good taste, but all the glowing colour of the old pictures, the soft gold of their frames, and the faded yellow damask had gone. The rooms no longer had that peaceful look which comes when the furniture had found and grown into its place through the centuries. Mr Cecil asked him to stay to tea, but he felt uneasy in the house, and said, as on his first visit, that he wanted to look at the village, and to ride back to Dilton before dark, as the bicycle had no lamp.

He went by the meadow path, first wheeling his bicycle across the lawn to the three oak trees. He stood by the bridge looking back at the house. At one time he had thought of Waterpark as his only real home. He had expected to spend his life there, married to Sylvia. He tried to imagine what that life would have been like, but his imagination could not work unless stimulated by his feelings, and he no longer had any feeling about this place. The ethos created by long association between one people and one stretch of land, or between a family and their dwelling place seemed to have evaporated. The tie which bound his blood to this land had broken. It had not snapped suddenly, but the cord had slowly perished, and now fallen soundlessly apart.

When he did succeed in imagining that Mr Cecil had ended his tenancy, and that he had inherited the place, he had a feeling of oppression. He thought of all he would have to do if he lived there, and with insufficient money. He would have to bring back the furniture and the pictures from Australia again, those unfortunate ancestors who at intervals were transported across the Indian Ocean. The thought was a nightmare.

He stood on the bridge looking down into the stream where as children they had played through the long summer days among the reeds, becoming almost part of its intimate life of frogs and dragonflies. Here his brother Bobby, now nearly twenty years dead, had held his imaginary conversations with the trout, while his grandparents and parents in their easy-going way had laughed and gossiped as they sat at tea under the oak trees. These memories could not evoke them. Here they were an idea, not an emotion, and he thought of them as leading their true life in the Australian countryside. He felt as he had in the hollow room in the hospital, that the life and colour were gone. This was partly because he felt that something was gone from himself.

He rode his bicycle across the narrow meadow path, where so often in the early days of summer, the buttercups had filled the creases in his shoes with yellow dust as he walked on his way to see Colonel Rodgers, for one of those sessions with guns and swords, to sit entranced while the colonel told him of battles and bullfights, of the thousands of birds and animals he had shot, and how he had killed the two natives whose shrunken mummified heads were his *garniture de cheminée*. Instinctively he went to the church to look once more at the tombs, which, apart from

Cousin Emma, and the colonel in the War Office, and that young widowed cousin in Dorset whom he had not yet been to see, contained almost the only relatives he had in England. The earlier tombs were under simple stone slabs let into the floor. In the seventeenth century they had become more ostentatious, and there were wall monuments with skulls, cherubs and coats-of-arms. No Langtons had been buried here for two generations. The last was Cousin Thomas, to whose memory his grandfather had put up that window blazing with escutcheons. As a boy he had been proud of its brilliance and grandeur. Now it had no meaning for him. It was as if he had come across one of his old toys, a wooden horse pulled on wheels. Or, if it had a meaning it was a deathly one, not because it was a memorial to the dead, but because all those shields were themselves part of the panoply of battle and murder and sudden death. They should be taken from the church, as the pictures had been taken from Hermione's dining-room, to make it a place of healing.

Yet how had he felt in that hollow room? More deathly than peaceful, with its breathing colour gone. Was it possible that the only things that coloured his own life, that made his blood flow, were in themselves deathly? That if they were removed he would be as empty as that ward, as bleak as this church would be if the armorial tombs and the glowing window were taken away? He began to feel the stoppage in his brain, and before that dreadful feeling completely possessed him he left the church which had brought it on.

He rode hurriedly through the village, not staying to see Colonel Rodgers as he had intended. He wanted to escape the past. It seemed to him that all the beauty of the English countryside contained within itself a single evil, the obsession with killing. All the life he had enjoyed, all his amusements were centred on killing. The chapel of the most gracious country house, of Waterpark itself, peaceful and secluded with its lichened stone, its lawns, its stream, its cooing doves, was really the gun-room.

## CHAPTER ELEVEN

THE HOME FOR SHELL-SHOCKED OFFICERS WAS TO the east of Marazion, on the south-west slope of a hill. It had been built by a retired tea-planter from India, and designed to trap as much sun as possible in a northern climate. There was a verandah with a wide balcony over it, which could be enclosed with glass in the winter. From this there was a clear view of the sea and of St Michael's Mount, but of the side away from Penzance. Dominic arrived in the evening and the castle was against the light of the setting sun, still mysterious, still Wagnerian.

He dined in a sort of mess for the patients. They all seemed a little odd to him, nervous, despondent or excitable; but he supposed that he was a little odd himself. The worst cases did not come in to meals, but had them in their rooms, and these were given single rooms. Dominic was also given a single room. He often found that in life, for no apparent reason, he was allowed privileges, but now it was because of his association with Lord Dilton. He went up immediately after dinner to settle himself in, and to write to Helena, telling her where he was. He said that he was quite fit, but that "they" thought he should come here for a time. He did not mention his attitude to the war, nor his intentions. He could not explain them in a letter. He would do so when he returned; and he thought that she who stood for all that was best in his life, who was so good and sane and kind and wholesome would naturally accept them, and that they would be drawn together again closer than ever, in body and spirit. He could not even hint at this in a letter. He told her that he would not be sent back to France, so that she should not be anxious about him.

His room was at the end of a row which opened through glass doors on to a balcony. When he came up from breakfast he stepped out to look at the view of the sea and the castle in the morning light. Sitting in a cane chair outside the window next to his own was a young man with the most evil and hideous face he had ever seen. The mouth would not close over the teeth and was twisted in a cruel sneer. The cheek had a kind of knotted lump in it, and from an almost lidless eye-socket stared a blue blank glass eye. Dominic felt shocked and sick, and stepped back quietly into his room, before the other could be aware of him.

He sat on his bed for a minute, and then rose to go down to the ground floor verandah. The stairs were at the far end of the passage, and from the landing another glass door led on to the balcony. He went through it to look at the view thinking that he would be able to avoid seeing the young man at the far end. He leaned on the rail looking down at the deep, greeny-purple sea. It was a fine morning at the end of October, and the white horses of the breaking waves gleamed in the misty sunlight, which now shone too in its morning freshness on St Michael's Mount. When he saw it he thought of Sylvia, but in this light he did not recall the wild desires of the room in Penzance. He took in deep breaths of the strong air, and felt as if he were freeing himself from the fumes of a narcotic. He turned to enter the house again, but could not prevent his eyes glancing along the balcony to that dreadful figure, still staring out at the sea.

At first he thought that another young man had taken its place, or that he himself was suffering from an hallucination. He stood still with surprise, not only at the change, but at the distinction of the face he now saw, which, even more surprisingly, seemed vaguely familiar. Then he realized that it was Hollis.

He went down the balcony and spoke his name.

Hollis did not turn his face towards him, but he moved his eye to see who had spoken. When he saw Dominic he exclaimed: "Langton!" and took his hand, holding it in a tight grip which he would not release, as if he were being saved from drowning. A tear rolled from his eye down his cheek, its former schoolboy chubbiness now finely drawn with suffering, and beautiful in its sad contours.

Dominic said: "I'll get a chair from my room," and made to step round him, but Hollis swiftly turned his head away and said: "Please don't go on that side of me. You can go through my room." His voice was a little slurred.

Dominic did not know whether to tell him that he had already seen the other side of his face, and to pretend that it was not so bad; but he did not yet feel sufficiently steeled to keep up his pretence. He brought his cane chair round through Hollis's room and sat beside him. When they had sufficiently expressed their surprise at finding themselves together again, Dominic told him how he had come to be there, but did not tell him his ideas about the war, partly because of Hollis's condition. He soon found that everything to do with the cause of his disfigurement was a horror to him, and he had developed an almost uncanny animal sensitiveness and agility in keeping the wounded side of his face from the view of anyone but the doctor and nurse. He ate with difficulty and was one of those allowed their meals in their rooms.

They talked of the more trivial pleasant times they had had in France, of meals in hotels, but not of the dinner on the night when Hollis had visited the prostitute. Hollis recalled how one morning, after a fortnight in the mud of the trenches, his boots had been bleached of all colour. His servant had cleaned them with "oxblood" polish, and he had gone on parade with bright pink boots. He laughed at this memory. It was one of the few amusing incidents he was treasuring to support him through the rest of his life when nothing funny could happen. He would tell it for another forty years. His laughter had a curious sound because of the injury to his mouth.

Dominic after an hour's conversation felt drained of vitality. He found that all the time he had been making the pretence that everything was normal and agreeable, and that it was a pleasure for them to be there. It was perhaps a pleasure for Hollis that he had come, if it can be called a pleasure when a starving man is given a crust of bread. For Dominic was only a crust from the full life he had known, and to him it was no pleasure to sit by this boy who had been, and was in a different way still his friend, and to know that he dared not look at the other side of that beautiful profile. All the time he was trying to shut it out of his imagination. Also Hollis's cheerfulness was false. It was febrile, a pretence that what he had lost still existed.

A nurse released him by saying that the doctor was ready to see him. The doctor gave him a brief overhaul and said, in a puzzled way: "You're as fit as a fiddle, and your nerves seem all right. Why have they sent you here?"

"It's really because of what I think," said Dominic uncertainly.

"What you think? What d'you mean?"

"When I think of going back to the war I get a kind of jam in my brain." He knew he had expressed this as badly as possible, but the doctor's manner rattled him.

"You mean you've got cold feet."

Dominic felt a surge of anger, an impulse that he had not experienced since he was wounded.

The doctor muttered something, took up a paper and read out: "Shell-shock." Then he said: "Very well. That's all for the present."

Dominic walked up the hill behind the house. He was trembling with his controlled impulse of violence. He sat down on a stone to try to calm himself. He had thought that the violence in his nature had fused, but it had flickered again in a sudden sharp red light. He felt the same impulse as when he had sent a challenge to Harrison. He had thought that his honour demanded that. But it was an artificial honour.

Now the coat-of-arms had gone with the rest of the colour from his traditional room. He felt an awful sense of disintegration. He was trying to reason about things in his nature which he could not understand. He looked down at the white hospital, and from above could see the striped roof of the balcony. He thought of Hollis sitting there, hiding half his face. He thought of the German boy. He had resolved that he would never send another body rolling on the ground, and that through him no other Hollis should spend his life in a torment of division. That was enough. It was futile to reason about it. He could only stick to his decision whatever happened.

Away to his right, beyond the house, the noonday sun shone on the island mountain, the church and the castle, beautiful but simple facts, no longer a mystery. It was what he required of life, beauty and simplicity, not mystery. He did not want to feel this endless agonized yearning for what he could not understand, the feeling he had when he made love to Sylvia, against the castle and the sea. He tried to imagine her with him now, and only knew that if she were, he would want to escape.

In the afternoon he went again to see Hollis, who asked him if he would come for a walk with him after tea, when it would be dark. He left his end of the balcony only after sunset, when the other patients were in the dining-room dawdling over their tea. Hollis said that he would meet him at the front door at five o'clock.

When Dominic came he was standing out in the dusk, with the right side of his face turned to him. He had pulled his hat down over the left side which gave him a jaunty appearance, but somehow this combination of jauntiness with the infinitely sad beauty of his profile made him appear sinister.

They walked along the coast road. He kept Dominic on his right, and when they turned, with that almost animal instinctive agility, he kept the left side of his face always hidden.

Hollis began to talk about the woman he had visited in Béthune. She had already become for him the symbol of freedom and abundant life. He had forgotten her slight irritability and his dissatisfaction afterwards. He spoke of her emotionally.

"I think of her as my wife," he said, "she is the only one I shall ever have."

Dominic was silent. He could not tell him that he too had visited that woman. It would be like telling him that he had seduced his wife, if that was what she had become in his mind. It would be destroying this vision of what he had to feed on all his life as his experience of marriage. When they returned to the house it was dinnertime, and they parted for the night.

6+w.b.s.                                                      [161]

For dinner there was some twice-cooked mince, floury potatoes hard in the middle, and a steamed suet pudding. This, after the perfectly cooked fresh food at Dilton, upset Dominic's stomach; and it was eaten in the company of men all suffering from disordered nerves, instead of in the tranquil magnificence of the Dilton dining-room. The man opposite him could not stop twitching.

He went early to bed but could not sleep. He thought of Hollis living for life on the memory of half an hour with a prostitute, his whole intimate experience of "love". He thought of his own visit to the woman and wondered how he could ever have gone there. It was, he believed, because everything that he had done from the moment he had returned from leave till the moment he was wounded was evil.

It was evil because he had performed what in nature were hot-blooded actions in cold blood. The devil was not hot but cold. He had deliberately in cold blood taken the idea of violence into his mind, knowing from his dream in the train what he was doing. In cold blood he had given that filthy talk on violence to his men. He had obeyed the instruction to keep alive the spirit of the offensive, when the spirit of the offensive was cold. He had visited that woman in cold blood. It was because his blood was cold that he waited that split second while the German soldier ran him through with his bayonet, and he had received the reward of his actions.

As he lay awake the events of the past few months passed in disturbed sequence through his mind. He thought of Sylvia and St Michael's Mount, and of Hollis sitting on the balcony looking at it from the other side, and he realized that if Hollis had not been wounded he might not have been in Cornwall with Sylvia. It was Hollis's wound that advanced his leave, so that it did not clash with Maurice's.

It was a strange coincidence, a bizarre design of life, that he was now here with Hollis. When at last he fell asleep he had confused nightmares in which the two different aspects of St Michael's Mount had become the two sides of Hollis's face, and Sylvia was the whore of Béthune. Everything was split and double.

After a few days he fell into a routine. He spent his time exclusively with Hollis, not only because their earlier friendship enabled them to talk unreservedly, but also because Hollis was the only one in the house whose nerves were not disordered. He was full of sorrow, sometimes inclined to be morbid, but so far sane.

They played games together, draughts, chess and two-handed poker. Dominic bought beer in the village, and they sat on the balcony, smoking, drinking and playing cards in a kind of continuation of their life in the mess. It was against the rules to bring drink into the home, but again a freedom was allowed to Dominic which others could not have taken, perhaps because the nurses favoured him for his looks. However, the doctor spoke to him sharply about his exclusive association with Hollis, saying it was abnormal.

"He was in my regiment," said Dominic, "we were in France together. Besides he can't talk to anyone else."

"He could if he wanted to," said the doctor. "It's only vanity."

Again Dominic felt his fused violence flickering back to life. Before it blazed he turned and walked out of the room. Was Hollis to be allowed nothing, was he to be deprived of the only facet he could present to the world, the illusion that he was still a healthy and handsome boy? And yet Dominic was uneasy. There was something in the way Hollis cherished the illusion, in the instinctive animal agility of his concealment that was perhaps abnormal.

Then he thought: "Damn it! What right have they to expect him to be 'normal' when they have done that to his face?" Illusion was all that was left to him.

One night when they were walking it was very dark. They did not speak much. After a while Dominic asked quietly: "Why won't you let me see all your face?"

"You know why. The other side is like hell," said Hollis.

"I would soon get used to it."

"You couldn't. I wouldn't want you to. I wouldn't want you to think of me like that."

"I would know that was not you. I would still have the other side where I can see you truly."

"You couldn't help yourself. The bad side makes the most impact."

"It shouldn't. I feel that the concealment makes a kind of constraint between us."

"No one can reveal himself wholly to another person, although you know more of me than anyone else does. Another thing, if you were a bit irritated with me, as you are sometimes when I'm slow making a move in chess, and if you looked up then and saw my face, you would hate me."

"I couldn't hate you," said Dominic seriously.

Hollis did not reply, and Dominic felt that the tears were welling from his eye – perhaps from that awful blind socket.

Christmas came and they had painful festivities. The disordered men with forced hilarity hung up mistletoe and holly in the dining-room. Their relatives sent crystallized fruit and crackers, which could not be pulled, as in one or two of the patients any explosion produced a state of panic. One of the local families sent them brandy, which again was forbidden. Dominic wanted to eat his Christmas dinner with Hollis in his room, partly so that he should not be alone, and also to avoid the pretence of merriment downstairs. But Hollis would not hear of it. He would not let anyone see him eat.

Dominic sent a Christmas card to the Diltons, and he wrote as well to Lord Dilton saying that he was very fit, but still held the same attitude to the war. He said that he was receiving no treatment of any kind, mental or physical. He did not see that he could stay in the hospital indefinitely. Lord Dilton replied asking him to put up with it a little longer.

After Christmas Dominic and Hollis fell back into their former routine. Often they could only take short walks after tea because of the bad weather. When they became tired of games they talked and talked. Dominic told Hollis of the resolution he had made. He was not shocked but he was uninterested. It was now outside the scope of his own life. Dominic quoted to him what he had read about the good man and the bad man in the library at Dilton, but he only said: "I suppose so." Although he had said that no man can reveal himself wholly to another man, there was little of himself that he did not reveal on these dark evenings, either sitting in his little room with his face averted, or walking along the road above the winter sea.

Their intimacy was now so complete that one night Dominic told him that he had visited the woman in Béthune.

"D'you mean just to talk?" asked Hollis.

"No," he replied.

Hollis did not seem upset. Perhaps his imaginative picture of this woman had changed. He had not mentioned her recently. But the next night when they were again out walking he referred to her. It was a mild February night, the sky was full of stars and there was a feeling in the air that soon the trees would blossom.

"D'you remember that night when we were walking back," asked Hollis, "and the orchard?"

"Yes," said Dominic, but he did not want to talk about it. Two or three times in his life he had had this impulse to strip himself and walk naked under the stars in some remote sylvan place – along an Australian bush road, on a cliff above Port Phillip Bay, and then, so much later, in the orchard near Béthune. He did not know why he obeyed this impulse, which had sometimes equally been felt by saints and poets. At the time it gave him a feeling of serenity, that with his clothes all evil was shed away. When he remembered it afterwards he was ashamed, because of the puritan instruction of his childhood. Hollis apparently wanted to talk of it, but Dominic was not responsive.

The days grew longer and it was light again after tea. Hollis would not walk out until after dinner, when in his jaunty hat he waited for Dominic at the front door. As they walked along the coast road he again referred to the orchard near Béthune, and said that soon the trees would be in blossom.

"Not the apples," said Dominic.

"The plum trees will soon be out," Hollis replied. "They will look wonderful in the moonlight. There will be a full moon in a fortnight." This evening the moon was a pale crescent, just above the tower of the castle.

A night or two later he led the way along a road beyond St Hilary, where he said that there was an orchard.

"What sort of trees are they?" asked Dominic to humour him, yet he felt in himself a faint interest, almost an excitement at the image of the orchard in bloom. But it was not an impulse towards innocence, which had made him walk along the bush track in his boyhood.

The orchard was on a southern slope, and was of mixed trees, apples, pears and plums, the latter with swelling buds, and a few in this sheltered place already showing tips of white.

"You see," said Hollis. "They will be out at the full moon."

After this on every walk he spoke of the coming full moon. It was impossible to keep him away from the subject. It had become an obsession with him, a morbid compensation. He spoke as if it had implications of which they were both aware. At times Dominic had the feeling that he must escape, that he could not stand this routine any longer – the walks always in the darkness, and always with that beautiful profile turned to him, and the other hideous side of the face concealed beneath the jaunty hat. At other times he felt himself touched with the same morbidity, and when Hollis counted the days to the full moon, he shared his excitement that they were few. But he knew that this orchard would not be the same as that near Béthune. Then his impulse had been towards innocence, rising in the heart. This would be planned in the head, and he knew that when actions which normally sprang from the heart were planned, they were tainted.

They came in one night, and when he parted from Hollis at the door of his room, he knew that he was committed to this rendezvous in the orchard. In his own room he had a sudden violent reaction, an enlightenment. He rubbed the palms of his hands in his eyes. He was living in a madhouse and he had let it infect him. Everything here was double and confused. Even the view of St Michael's Mount had become a sort of hallucination of duality, which had its exact and dreadful counterpart in Hollis's face. Outside of this place Venus and Mars had kept their separate identities, but here they were united into a horrible hermaphrodite. He had to get away at any cost. It was better to be imprisoned or shot than to be touched with madness. He sat down and wrote to Lord Dilton saying that he must leave the hospital at once, even if it meant court martial. In a moment of desperation he added a postscript that he would come back to the depot if he could escape from this place.

In the morning he re-read his letter. Its tone was urgent but there was nothing he wanted to alter, though he was uneasy about the postscript. He was going to cross it out, but did not do so because he thought it would look untidy, and after all surely anything was better than to rot into lunacy. After breakfast he walked down to the village to post the letter himself in the same way that he had gone out to post his letter to Lord Dilton from the Mayfair hotel. He wanted to be sure that it went, and as soon as possible.

When he came back the second post had arrived, and amongst the letters on the baize board was one for himself from Lord Dilton. He wished that he had not been so hurried in posting his own letter. As he was opening the envelope, a nurse came and told him that the doctor wanted to see him. He went to the office, or surgery.

"You're invalided out," said the doctor. "I'm damned if I know why. It's not my doing. Anyhow you're free to go when you like."

Dominic was dazed. He walked slowly upstairs. At first he wished more strongly that he had not posted that letter, especially that he had not written the postscript. On the landing he read Lord Dilton's letter, which also told him that he was invalided out, and gave him some instructions. But he was free – that was the main thing. He could go at once, this afternoon. He would escape another of those night walks with Hollis when most he felt that his sanity was in danger. When he thought of that he had a great affection and pity for Hollis. He went out on to the balcony to tell him. He was sitting waiting with a chess board ready on the wicker table.

"Where have you been?" he asked fretfully. "It's going on for eleven o'clock."

"I've been out to post a letter."

"You could have put it in the box in the hall."

"It was important. I've been invalided out. I'm leaving this afternoon."

Hollis sat perfectly still. He did not speak for a minute. Then tears welled from his eye and rolled down his sad beautiful cheek. Dominic was moved. He had not known anyone weep at losing him before. Even Helena, if she had wept, had kept her tears till he had gone. And yet he was himself full of relief and gladness, even at leaving Hollis. He wanted to make some compensation to him.

"I wish you could leave too," he said feebly, "and get away from all this." Suddenly Hollis turned his full face to him. The tears too were welling from under the staring glass eye, and running down the twisted hollows of his cheek. Dominic tried to keep any shock of repulsion from showing in his face, and so deprived it of all expression. It was clear that Hollis expected some response, some action from him. His living eye looked up, accusing and appealing. Dominic did not know what response to make. He put out his hand uncertainly. Hollis did not take it, but turned his face away again, and seemed to ignore his presence.

Dominic said: "I'll go and pack." There was now no reason why he should not walk past Hollis, but he kept to the former convention and went round through the other bedroom to his own.

He had a dreadful feeling of inadequacy. He should have said something, done something that Hollis expected. Should he like St Francis have bent and kissed that hideous cheek? Then he thought what a beastly thing that would have been – when the boy offered him his whole face, to kiss only the side that was distorted and horrible, ignoring what he still had of life and health, the smooth fresh skin of his youth. And that was what everyone was doing. They would only caress youth when it was wounded. The whole and the sane must pass first through the Moloch jaws. With anger he thought of Sylvia at Victoria Station, and her question to the subaltern: "Have you been over the top yet?"

He spent the rest of the morning packing. After lunch he went out on to the balcony to spend with Hollis the twenty minutes or so before he left, but now they found little to say.

When Dominic stood up to go he said: "Show me all your face."

Hollis at first stiffened into rigid obstinacy. Then, not with a sudden defiance as in the morning, but slowly he turned showing his full face. Dominic stroked gently his smooth unblemished cheek. A look of surprise and then almost of happiness came into Hollis's eye, as if something had been restored to him. When Dominic entered the car, waiting in the drive below, he came to the edge of the balcony and called goodbye to him, looking directly down at him.

From the train Dominic saw St Michael's Mount from yet another angle. Under the grey sky it looked picturesque with the fishermen's cottages at its base, but with no suggestion of mystery. All the same he wished that he had gone there, and climbed up to the castle on the summit. It would have been simpler than he had imagined, as now it was low tide he saw that the Mount was joined to the mainland by a causeway.

# CHAPTER TWELVE

FOLLOWING THE INSTRUCTIONS IN LORD DILTON'S letter, Dominic went up to London to complete the formalities of his demobilization. A passage back to Melbourne had been arranged for him, and the ship left in ten days' time. There was no suggestion that he should come to Dilton before leaving England, and it was clear that he was expected to go without any more fuss. The letter concluded with formal good wishes for his complete restoration to health.

Lord Dilton's attitude to Dominic had changed, not only because of the failure of his plan; though if he did not succeed in an object he preferred to blot it out of his mind as soon as possible. He began this process as soon as he had written his final instructions to Dominic. When he had his letter asking to be released at any cost from the hospital he glanced through it, thought with impatience: "That's all done with," and threw it into the waste-paper basket. He hardly took in the implications of Dominic's desperate postscript, offering to return to the depot. He did not want him back. He was too unpredictable. He felt towards him much as he had after his broken engagement to Sylvia. It was possible that if they met in another five years' time their latent friendship might reawaken. At the moment he did not want to see him.

But the deepest cause of his change of attitude was something outside themselves. It was now March 1918 and the Germans had begun their offensive. The English Fifth Army was cracking up. Béthune, like many other towns, became mostly ruins, the churches and the brothels heaps of rubble. Whatever Lord Dilton might have thought about passing an endless stream of young men into the Moloch jaws of the stationary trenches, now in a time of real danger, he thought such ideas treasonable. It was not a time when his patient treatment of Dominic could be extended. He still acted with concern for his welfare, but as much in his own interest as in Dominic's. He did not want to have the discredit of a rebellious officer in the battalion he commanded. The authorities did not want the bad propaganda of a decorated officer's being court-martialled for refusing to serve any further. The fact that he was an Australian made the situation more complicated. The best thing for everyone was to send him back to the bush as quietly as possible. Lord Dilton had pulled his strings with the greatest ease.

Dominic stayed alone in the little Mayfair hotel until the day of his departure. As when he was last there, he did not go to see any of the people whom he might have visited. He went to the War Office and to Cox's bank to complete his formalities, and spent the rest of his time walking about the streets. He felt as if he had climbed out too far along a branch, and was perched there isolated. If he had known the people who might have sympathized with his attitude, the socialistic pacifists, he would have shocked them with his Tory-anarchism, with his background of tradition, even if he had stripped away all its colour. His instincts were non-political. He had no ideas of progress through politics. He only wanted to achieve some passionate innocence in his own life, and to redeem his inherited violence, though this longing was not explicit in his mind.

All the time he was aware that he was close to Sylvia, but he did not want to see her. Sometimes he felt that by now her father would have told her all about him, and that she would meet him with the same insolence that she had shown to the subaltern at Victoria. At times he was filled with uneasiness, remembering the postscript to his letter to Lord Dilton. He knew that it was not true that he could have returned to his duties at the depot. He thought that this postscript must be the reason why Lord Dilton had not written to him again.

His ship sailed from Plymouth. On the evening before it left, he again took a train from Paddington, perhaps, he thought, for the last time. He had a sense of ending, of everything being for the last time. It was not oppressive, but only faintly melancholy. This was the station from which he had made so many fateful journeys – first as an infant from Australia being brought to live with his grandparents at Waterpark; then when his parents came back to take their inheritance; then when he had to go down to announce to them that he had failed for the army; then to join the regiment at the depot; then with Sylvia on their stolen honeymoon; then to convalesce at Dilton, and at the madhouse near Marazion; now finally to return to Australia, perhaps for good. He might never take another train from Paddington.

On the ship he entered that strange dream-like existence between two worlds. He now thought of Australia as his home. He had sweated Europe out of his system, and had done so with his blood. He had left the traditional room. His place was out in the open, in the natural world where Helena was waiting for him. That was the only place where he had come to terms with life.

The people on the ship were mostly Australians. There were some wounded men, invalided out like himself, but with more obvious reasons; and women more or less of the smart kind, wives of the wounded officers or vaguely connected with war work. Australia was his home, but he did not take in that these people were his fellow-countrymen, and that with them his sense of home-coming should begin. There was not the same hearty compulsion to games as on the voyage to England, but now, with a different reason, he kept to himself. Like Mrs Heseltine, but with less intelligent kindness, a gossipy woman tried "to take an interest in him". She said that she had had a wonderful time in London, doing war work in exalted circles.

"You must hate having to go back before it's all over," she said. "I expect you had tremendous fun."

Occasionally Dominic did feel discomfort that he was returning at this time, when the English army was in retreat, but he had never been much aware of the general progress of the war, in the way that Colonel Rodgers and the country clergymen followed it, pinning their flags into maps. The junior officers, Harrison, Frost, Raife, all of them were only concerned with their immediate line of trench and the routine connected with it. The rest was someone else's affair.

The gossipy woman gave him up, saying to her friends: "He looks marvellous, but he's as dull as ditchwater."

He did not mind. He thought of life ahead and Helena waiting for him. They would live at peace together, eating the fruit of their own vine, and no one else would matter. Their children would grow up in the innocence of the natural world. He elaborated his dream during the weeks of the voyage. He re-read Helena's letters, the detailed descriptions of life on the farm, at last visualizing it with the full force of his imagination.

He left the ship at Melbourne, both so that he would arrive home sooner, and also to see his parents. His father met him at Port Melbourne, to drive him to an uncle's house in South Yarra, where his mother was waiting. He was surprised at the expression of his father's face, welcoming him across the barrier at the end of the pier – the suppressed joy and relief of his son's returning alive from the war. In spite of his unfailing patience and kindness towards him, of the same nature but more disinterested than Lord Dilton's, Steven had really believed that Dominic disliked him. When Dominic met his mother she seemed both strange and familiar to him. The laws of gravity had once more changed. The air was light and unreal. After an hour or so they fell into their old easy way of talking. They did not mention the war or the reasons for his return, but they asked him a good many questions about Waterpark, and whether he really wanted to return there to live. His father believed that those who had fought and had been wounded in the war were entitled to all the promises made to them, and he had discussed at length with his wife the possibility of uprooting themselves again, and changing the whole pattern of their lives to fulfil their obligations to their hero son. They were surprised at the vehemence of his reply. They appeared to have stirred up some deep repugnance in him.

"No! Good heavens, no!" he exclaimed, and they exchanged a glance of relief, though of rueful amusement that they had wasted so many anxious hours discussing it.

In the evening there was a crowded family party, at which Dominic, the black sheep of more than twenty years, was the centre of admiration; though his Aunt Mildred made a great fuss because he was not in uniform. At intervals her voice could be heard bleating plaintively: "Oh, I *am* disappointed."

He met people whom he had not seen since he ran off with Helena and who, if it had not been for the war, would never have spoken to him again. He took their interest as a display of family affection, and not due to the fact that he had won the Military Cross, and had lost four pints of blood. Even less did he realize that if they knew what had brought him back so soon, half of them would not have come.

The next day he took the train to Sydney, and from there another train to the country station, twenty miles from his home, where Helena was to meet him in a Ford car recently given her by her mother. Before, they had used only horses. She had not gone down to Melbourne or even to Sydney, as she did not want their reunion to be amongst a crowd of relatives, or in a noisy city, but in the surroundings of their happy life together, which she had tried so hard in her letters to keep before him.

He put his head out of the carriage window a mile before the train reached the little wayside station. Here the country was flat, and the line ran straight ahead. Soon he could see a handful of tiny figures on the platform. He stared at them until he could distinguish a woman, standing a little apart, and knew that it must be Helena. He felt almost nervous and his heart beat quickly. At last he saw her clearly, in a tweed skirt, a white blouse and a hat like a man's. She walked along the platform to where he was leaning out of the window. He had to take his luggage from the train before he could greet her, as it had stopped only to drop him.

Then he turned to look at her. She too was strange, and yet familiar and kind. She was very brown. Her skin was not as smooth and cared for as when he left, and there was a mark on her cheek, a tiny scar left by the disease she had caught when dipping the sheep, and her eyelids had tired lines. She looked in some way a little harder, yet her eyes when she met his were so kind. He kissed her cheek and he felt that it was her kindness that he was kissing.

They turned towards the exit, where a little Union Jack was stuck over the door. When the train had drawn out, the station-master came up and greeted him, shaking his hand warmly and making a little speech of welcome. He beckoned to the other men to come up and shake hands, which they did with off-hand embarrassment.

The station-master helped them out with his luggage. Helena asked Dominic if he would like to drive, but he had not driven since he had occasionally been allowed to use his father's car at Waterpark eight years ago. Mr Gowrie, the station-master, made another speech about the wife holding the fort while the husband was away, but when he returned, the husband must take command. In spite of this Helena moved her brown tweed jacket from the driving seat and took the wheel. When she had driven half a mile she stopped the car and turned toward him.

They looked at each other, each seeking under the changes of these violent years the separated lover. She looked at him a little anxiously, searching with her eyes. He felt that she had changed, but only on the surface. She felt that there was some change in him at a deeper level. She missed something in him, the fire which it had been her pride to control. She thought perhaps it was only that he had become re-anglicized, conventionalized by the life of an English officer, and that back on the farm he would become his impulsive self again.

With tenderness for her kindness and loneliness he took her in his arms and they hugged each other tightly, desperately seeking their former selves. When he released her, she wiped her eyes with her handkerchief, and they drove on across the brown plains, between smooth brown hills, strangely capped with the white arabesques of white dead gum trees. There was not a drought, but the dry summer grass had not yet turned green with rain. After a while, to break the constraint of silence after their embrace, she said: "Why aren't you in uniform?" She did not say it critically, like Mrs Cecil and Colonel Rodgers, or fretfully like Aunt Mildred, but the question startled him.

"I'm no longer a soldier," he replied.

"But surely you could have been allowed to wear it till you got home."

"I don't know." He did not want to think about anything to do with the army. All that cult of death was over for him. He realized how utterly he had repudiated it when he did not go to see Colonel Rodgers on that last day at Waterpark. Helena was to restore him to life and innocence. That was the role he had fixed for her when he sat dreaming in his deckchair on the voyage out. Perhaps it was the role he had intended for her during the whole of his absence. He did not want her even to mention the army and the war, until the time came for him to explain to her that the traditional room in which he had lived was stripped of its furnishings, hollow and dead.

At last they came over a hill and saw below them the farm which he had longed for so impossibly when he was away, that at times it had seemed only to exist as a vision. Now it was a solid material reality, and Helena said: "Here we are."

He said: "Stop again," and she pulled up just below the brow of the hill. He wanted to look at his home before he reached it, to realize its actuality, to shed that feeling which again had come over him that the laws of gravity had changed and that he was light-headed. The white road curved down the hill to the little settlement, the white-painted house showing through the trees. The afternoon shadow was moving down the smooth hill, as cleanly as the sweep of a brush of water-colour, but the farm was still in the sunlight, the yellow trees and the orchard and the two poplars flanking the gate into the stableyard.

He wanted to realize that it was his, this lovely quiet place, and that he need never leave it again. Amongst those trees his own son was waiting for him, his wife was beside him; all these immense riches, all that a sane man could desire, were restored to him. Trying to realize it, to force himself to know it in his blood, he turned again and took Helena in his arms.

Stevie, their boy, was waiting on the verandah with Helena's one domestic, a girl called Effie. He came forward shyly, led by the pleasant-faced girl. He had been told that he must say: "Daddy" when he met Dominic, but he turned his head away.

"Go on," said Effie, nudging him.

The boy said: "Daddy" very quietly, looking the other way. They all laughed and Dominic picked him up. Stevie was not frightened of him, and soon was quiet and friendly. Dominic felt again the emotions he had when he held his new-born baby. Everything now was born again, restored to him in a way he had never imagined.

Stevie held Dominic's hand as they walked round the place, looking at improvements Helena had made, the extension of the garden, the new trees in the orchard, the new garage and the extra tanks. Everything was in perfect order, the grass mown, the beds weeded, the dead heads cut off every plant. They had all been slaving, since the day they heard that he had sailed, to make the place fit to welcome him. At last he had a welcome home, such an important thing in his life, equal to his expectations.

They had tea on the verandah, where the Gloire de Dijon was in thick bloom, and tangled with it were hanging purple grapes, and trees laden with ripe peaches and nectarines. Effie, whom from natural kindness and commonsense, but also from necessity, Helena had made a friend, sat with them and looked after the boy. Dominic felt that his life was restored to its pattern, simple and patriarchal. He wished that Harry, whom Helena had sacked, were here. He could not bring himself to ask about him. When he thought of doing so he felt a slight discomfort, a faint echo of the jam in his brain, which had come on him in the London hotel and at Dilton.

That night he made love to Helena. It was not as it had been before they went away. Then they had been entirely one, and they sank together into the sleep of fulfilment. Now they lay silent, each not liking to assume that the other was awake. They thought that they had to get used to each other again, or that their union after so long had disturbed more than solaced them. Or was it only that? Soon Helena asked quietly: "Are you asleep?"

He answered: "No," without any hint of drowsiness.

Some minutes passed in which each was conscious of the other's alert mind. Then she asked: "Have you been unfaithful to me?"

"Yes," he said, after a brief hesitation.

She was silent again, but then said: "Can you tell me with whom?"

Again he hesitated a little longer before saying: "With a woman in Béthune."

"A prostitute?" she asked.

"Yes."

They lay silent again. He wanted to say he was sorry, but he could not bring himself to do so without telling her the whole truth, and he could not tell her about Sylvia. He knew that it would hurt her dreadfully, and that it would blight the life that had been restored to him. It would be bringing the past to destroy the present.

She said: "I don't mind if it was only a physical necessity."

"I suppose it was," said Dominic.

"But I wish you hadn't."

"Yes," he agreed.

They were silent again. The emotions which they had hidden and treasured for three years were brought out, but churned up and confused. They had to clear them to return to their old understanding.

With Sylvia the only real accord had been that of their bodies, so he had made violent love to her body to try to understand her, to learn her with his hands. He could not restore his understanding with Helena in this way. It had to come through their hearts and minds, then their bodies would be in obedient harmony.

The window was open to the night. There was not a breath of wind. The stillness was absolute and in it their quiet voices were loud. From the garden came aromatic country smells. He was where he had longed to be, lying beside his wife in his own home, where every condition was peaceful except that of their minds. He had to remove what he believed was really the cause of their disunity, something more serious and enduring than his escapade with Sylvia. Now, when they were open to each other, lying in the darkness, his brain stimulated and clear, was the time to do it.

"I have to tell you something," he said.

"What is it?" Her voice sounded apprehensive, and he had the fleeting thought that she expected him to tell her about Sylvia. But he answered: "I am quite well. There is nothing wrong with me physically."

"That is wonderful."

"Yes, but there was no need for me to come home."

"You deserved it. You had done wonderfully well at the front. I am so proud of you."

"Other people couldn't come. I came because I chose to. If I had not been a friend of Lord Dilton's I might be in prison or shot."

"I don't understand."

"I want to explain to you now. If you understand, everything will be all right again, the same as when we left – better, because we shall have more understanding."

He told her all that had happened to him from the time he returned from leave, to the front line – the dream in the train, the attempt to fight a duel with Harrison, the blood-lust harangue to the troops. The murmur of his voice was the only sound in the still night. There was not even a rustle in the garden, the fall of a leaf. When he came to the morning of the attack he paused. She was afraid that he was going to say that he had made some dreadful blunder, and that only Lord Dilton's protection had saved him from the punishments he had mentioned. Then he told her how he had exchanged the look of recognition with the German boy, and at the same time had shot him. He paused again, waiting for her comment.

"You couldn't help it," she said. "If you hadn't shot him he would have killed you."

"He mightn't have. Not if I had returned his glance, not if I had recognized his humanity."

"But if everyone behaved like that you couldn't fight a war," said Helena a little impatiently.

"That is what I mean," said Dominic.

He told her how he was wounded, and how in hospital, in his doped, half-conscious state, he had always seen the German boy's face, the eyes in their split second of surprise awakening to friendship. He described the ward in Hermione's house, the emptiness of the hollow room, stripped like his mind of all traditional pictures. He told her of his conversation with Lord Dilton in London, of his further convalescence in his house, of his shooting the pheasant. Finally he described the home near Marazion and Hollis's face.

"So you see," he ended, "I am not the same as when I left."

"It's all dreadful," said Helena. "But we have to win the war, and those things are unavoidable."

He saw that he had failed to awaken her imagination, and that she could not visualize what he described. He tried to influence her by more practical arguments and said that the war could be ended by agreement, and he quoted some of Lord Dilton's remarks on the war-leaders and the profiteers. He told her how he had said that the war was destroying the landed families, and that those who were most strident in prosecuting it were none of them men with an understanding of the structure of Europe. But now he was not speaking from his heart. He was only nagging at her with his mind, putting forward arguments which to himself were secondary.

"You are talking like those horrible Labour people," she said, "who voted against conscription."

"The Australian soldiers also voted against conscription," he replied. He repeated his argument that when one conscript attacked another, he was only attacking an artificial menace to himself. She was horrified. He was trying to destroy every belief that had supported her during these three years, that had enabled her to run the farm without him, to sack Harry and to dip the sheep herself, to do a hundred things which she would not have contemplated if they had not been necessary in this struggle for their country and their freedom. For Helena was constitutionally incapable of not believing what she was told by authority and by people obviously better informed than herself. She accepted the surface of what was presented to her. If she had spent time considering what was behind it she could not have led her brave active life. She thought of Dominic as the sun and centre of her life and like Lord Dilton, felt that there was "something in him" that other men had not got, but she did not think it was political intelligence, and the capacity to judge world affairs. She told herself that his mind must be affected, otherwise he would not have been sent to that home in Cornwall, and then invalided out. It did not occur to her that Dominic, the dunce and black sheep of the family, could possibly be someone of such potential embarrassment to the authorities that they were glad to let him go home.

She felt a heavy depression as if her limbs were of lead, lying heavily on the bed. She had him back, but with a disfigurement far worse than one to his body. Soon he fell asleep, tired with his journey, his love-making, and the effort of trying to explain himself to her. But she did not sleep for a long time, wondering if his mental affliction would show itself in other ways, or if under the quiet wholesome influences of this place, he would be cured.

In a few days they had resumed the routine of daily life which his absence had interrupted, and often they were happy together. But the unresolved difference remained between them. Sometimes she thought he was not afflicted in his mind, but only perverse. When the March offensive was halted, and the Germans in their turn were on the run, he was glad because it seemed that the war would soon be over, but he could not share her light-hearted cheerfulness. He saw in his mind the battlefield. At times she was angry with him for his perversity.

In July he received an envelope with an English stamp,

and was a little puzzled by the familiarity of the hand-writing. It had been some time on the way, as it had been originally addressed to Cox's bank, who had forwarded it to his London bank, who had sent it on here. It did not contain a letter, but only two cuttings from *The Times*. One read: "The Hon. Mrs Maurice Wesley-Maude gave birth to a son in London yesterday." On this was scribbled in the corner, "18th April".

The other was from the casualty list under "Died of wounds".

It read: "Wesley-Maude. On the 15th April 1918, Maurice Vavasour Wesley-Maude, D.S.O., Major —*nth* Hussars."

He looked again at the envelope and saw that it had the Dilton postmark. He thought that the cuttings were sent by Lady Dilton, whose handwriting, not unlike Sylvia's, he vaguely remembered from helping her address the envelopes. Actually they were from Sylvia.

When in November the Armistice was signed, he and Helena were united in their relief that the war was over, and her slightly different emphasis was unnoticeable. Sometimes after that, a reference to the war, each seeing it from a different angle, might cause a tiff, but on the whole they jogged along contentedly enough.

It was not until the following year that Dominic's war medals arrived, and with them his Military Cross, as he had not attended an investiture. He had ridden to the mail-box and on his return he hung the reins over a post at the gate, and walked through the garden to the verandah where Helena was sitting sewing. He handed her two letters and looked at the small, rather heavy parcel from the War Office.

"What is that?" she asked.

"I don't know. It may be my medals," he said.

"Oh!" Her face lighted up with interest.

Effie came out on to the verandah. "I think the cake's done, Mrs Langton," she said. "It's very brown on top."

"I'll come and look at it," said Helena, putting down her sewing. When she returned a few minutes later Dominic had gone to take his horse round to the stables. He took off the bridle and saddle by the harness room, and then with a halter led the horse out to the water-hole in the paddock, and stood beside it while it drank. When, dribbling, it backed up the clayey slope, he thought that he would not be riding again that day, so he slipped off its halter, and giving it a smack on the rump, let it go free.

Still standing by the pond, with the halter on his arm, he took the package of medals from his pocket and idly examined it, finally opening it with his pocket-knife. The two service medals were in a white cardboard box, the Military Cross in its separate case. He looked at them curiously. One of the medals was inscribed "The War for Civilization".

He stood a long time, holding it and looking at it, and while he did so he forgot the horse, grazing in the paddock a few yards from him; he forgot his home and his child, and his wife waiting for him on the verandah. All the things he had longed for vanished from his consciousness and he saw only the places where he had most sharply longed for them.

He saw it all again, but now without that numbness, the anaesthetic which nature provided to stop the soldiers going mad. Even when he had found Hollis in No-man's-land, twitching and gurgling with half his face a mass of blood, his mind refused to pass on to his heart what had happened. When he made his report to Harrison after blowing up the German dug-out, this anaesthetic had not completely worked. When the men had fallen over like dolls in the attack, he had felt no pity for them, only a curiosity at what was happening. Now, in contrast with this peaceful place, where the only sound was that of the horse cropping the grass, the immensity of the suffering of the war overwhelmed him, as when he tried to reason with Lord Dilton in the hotel sitting-room. These medals were given him for his share in inflicting that suffering, that agony multiplied and multiplied beyond the possibility of calculation. And this Military Cross was awarded for what to him was the worst thing he had ever done, when he had violated his own nature at its deepest level.

He gave a shudder of repudiation; and with an almost involuntary gesture, he flung the medals into the clayey-yellow pond. There was a splash of light where they hit the water, from the sunlight on the spray and from their own silver. As he watched the circle of ripples widen and die away, he was aware that he had put himself once more where he had been before this marriage to Helena, outside the fellowship of ordinary men.

He was partly shocked at himself. His native Toryism was shocked at his anarchy. He realized fully the implication of what he had done, that it was in a sense of repudiation of the social order as well as of the war. He felt utterly alone.

His face was heavy as he walked back to the house, the flesh seeming to sag on his bones, giving him that appearance of a skull, as when he had slept opposite Hollis in the train to Dover.

Helena had returned to the verandah. As he came up the path and she saw his expression, she gave a start.

"What is the matter?" she asked. "Where are the medals?"

"They are in the pond," said Dominic.

"Oh, how dreadful!" She rose quickly, and threw her sewing on to a chair.

"We must try to rake them out." She thought that he had ridden his horse into the water, and that they had fallen from his pocket.

"We can't. They're in the middle – I threw them there."

She looked at him with sudden apprehension. She half thought that he was joking, but it was not the kind of joke that he made. She used to understand him perfectly, the meaning of every movement and every inflection of his voice, but now she could no longer be sure. Something had happened to him, some transmutation of his nature. He was cold to all that warmed her heart, when before he had been its central flame. And he was cold too towards what was for her the noblest experience of mankind in their century. All through the war she had felt: "Now God be thanked who matched us with his hour." She firmly believed, and no one else whom she knew doubted it, that the war was a struggle not only for their survival, but for that of every decent human instinct. Their young men had bled and died for them, and Dominic dared to question the value of their sacrifice. All through the war she had stayed here in loneliness and hardship to keep the farm going, doing her small part to help those who were fighting evil, chiefly Dominic himself. And this was involved with a personal reason. They had been happy before the war, but it was happiness stolen illicitly by their elopement. After the war she had thought, they would have won it honourably.

Now he had made all her hope and all her activity senseless, as if she had been merely some busy but useless machine, pulling nothing. And if he had really thrown his medals into the pond, he had insulted the wounds of brave men, the tears of every bereaved mother, and the bodies of the dead.

"You're not serious?" she said.

# MORE ABOUT PENGUINS AND PELICANS

For further information about books available from Penguin please write to Dept EP, Penguin Books Ltd, Harmondsworth, Middlesex UB7 ODA.

*In the U.S.A.*: For a complete list of books available from Penguin in the United States write to Dept DG, Penguin Books, 299 Murray Hill Parkway, East Rutherford, New Jersey 07073.

*In Canada*: For a complete list of books available from Penguin in Canada write to Penguin Books Canada Ltd, 2801 John Street, Markham, Ontario L3R 1B4.

*In Australia*: For a complete list of books available from Penguin in Australia write to the Marketing Department, Penguin Books Australia Ltd, P.O. Box 257, Ringwood, Victoria 3134.

*In New Zealand*: For a complete list of books available from Penguin in New Zealand write to the Marketing Department, Penguin Books (N.Z.) Ltd, P.O. Box 4019, Auckland 10.

## PICNIC AT HANGING ROCK
*Joan Lindsay*

On a summer Saint Valentine's Day in the year 1900, a party of school girls from the fashionable Appleyard College at Macedon, Victoria set out to picnic beneath the Hanging Rock. Several members of the party are never to return, and countless exquisitely ordered lives are disrupted again and again by the mystery which menaces out of the Australian bush.

## TIME WITHOUT CLOCKS
*Joan Lindsay*

*Time Without Clocks* is the charming and evocative autobiography of Joan Lindsay. It is the story of her marriage to Daryl Lindsay, of their life in Melbourne during the twenties and thirties, their travels in Europe, and above all the gentle world of 'Mulberry Hill', a house without clocks.

Revealed in this delightful reminiscence is Joan Lindsay's fascination with the ambiguities of time, seen by some as the key to the mystery of *Picnic at Hanging Rock*.

## TIRRA LIRRA BY THE RIVER
*Jessica Anderson*

Life has become a series of escapes for Nora Porteous. The tightness of a small-town family life, a sanctimonious and mean-hearted husband, the torpor of suburbia – these she endures and finally escapes. On her flight from cruel realities she is sustained by desperate courage, discerning intelligence and ebullient humour. Spanning seventy odd years, the action moves from Brisbane to Sydney to London and back again. This is a beautifully realized novel, enriched by the bitter-sweet tang of the past.

## THE IMPERSONATORS
*Jessica Anderson*

Jack Cornock's illness, and his obstinate silence, provoke speculation about his will among the families of his two marriages. When his daughter Sylvia returns to Australia after twenty years, she is inevitably caught up in the twisted skeins of their allegiances and estrangements. Sensitively crafted, *The Impersonators* is a modern novel portraying with humour and perception the fracturing of family relationships and the endurance of love in an increasingly materialistic age.

'One of Australia's foremost writers, able to detail with compassion and clarity contemporary urban life in Australia'
*Sydney Morning Herald*

'An elaborately worked and richly rewarding comedy of manners'
*Adelaide Advertiser*

# A FRINGE OF LEAVES
*Patrick White*

With *A Fringe of Leaves* Patrick White has richly justified his Nobel Prize. Set in Australia in the 1840s, this novel combines dramatic action with a finely distilled moral vision. It is a masterpiece.

Returning home to England from Van Diemen's Land, the *Bristol Rose* is shipwrecked on the Queensland coast and Mrs Roxburgh is taken prisoner by a tribe of aborigines, along with the rest of the passengers and crew. In the course of her escape, she is torn by conflicting loyalties – to her dead husband, to her rescuer, to her own and to her adoptive class.

# THE VIVISECTOR
*Patrick White*

Hurtle Duffield loves only what he paints. The men and women who court him during his long life are, above all, the materials of his art. He is the Vivisector, dissecting their weaknesses with cruel precision: his sister's deformity, a grocer's moonlight indiscretion, the passionate illusions of such women as the sugar heiress Boo Davenport, and his mistress Hero Pavloussi, wife of a Greek shipping magnate. Only the egocentric adolescent he sees as his spiritual child elicits from him a deeper, more treacherous emotion.

In this prodigious novel about the life and death of a great painter, Patrick White illuminates creative experience with unique truthfulness.

# THE MERRY-GO-ROUND IN THE SEA
*Randolph Stow*

In 1941, when his admired twenty-year-old cousin Rick left to join the army, Ron Coram was six. Geraldton and the sheep stations owned by his numerous relatives formed his world. The war, remote in place and interest, seemed hardly farther away than Australia – a country Rob had heard of without realizing he lived there.

During the next eight years everything was to change for Rob. Rick came back from the war, disillusioned and restless. Rob himself began to outgrow the unquestioned beliefs of his family, yet realized with helpless love that much of what he was losing was to him most precious.

Semi-autobiographical, yet not a self-portrait, this story of a boy growing up as part of an Australian clan in a small town and the country around it marvellously evokes a sense of the identity of Australia, its history and fate.

# FLY AWAY PETER
*David Malouf*

For three very different people brought together by their love for birds, life on the Queensland coast in 1914 is the timeless and idyllic world of sandpipers, ibises and kingfishers.

In another hemisphere civilization rushes headlong into a brutal conflict. Life there is lived from moment to moment.

Inevitably, the two young men – sanctuary owner and employee – are drawn to the war, and into the mud and horror of the trenches of Armentières. Alone on the beach, their friend Imogen, the middle-aged wildlife photographer, must acknowledge for all three of them that the past cannot be held.

'The continuities of nature are set against the obscenities of war . . . to construct a memorable book'

*Sunday Telegraph*, London

'The novel of a poet without a single trace of overwriting'

*Daily Telegraph*, London

# CHILD'S PLAY
*David Malouf*

In the streets of an ordinary Italian town, the people go about their everyday lives. In an old apartment block above them, a young man pores over photographs and plans, dedicated to his life's most important project.

Day by day, in imagination, he is rehearsing for his greatest performance. Yet when his moment comes, nothing could have prepared him for what happens.

'One of the most effective and penetrating studies of the mind and being of a fanatic'.

*Financial Times*, London